The Military Family's Parent Guide for Supporting Your Child in School

Ron Avi Astor,
Linda Jacobson, Rami Benbenishty
Julie A. Cederbaum, Hazel R. Atuel, Tamika Gilreath,
Marleen Wong, Kris M. Tunac De Pedro,
Monica Christina Esqueda, and Joey Nuñez Estrada Jr.

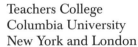

Teachers College
Columbia University
New York and London

Military Child Education Coalition®
909 Mountain Lion Circle
Harker Heights, TX 76548

This publication was developed by the USC Building Capacity in Military Connected Schools team, in part, with grant funds from the U.S. Department of Defense Education Activity under Award Number HE1254-10-1-0041. The views expressed in this profile do not necessarily reflect the positions or policies of the Department, and no official endorsement by the Department is intended or should be inferred.

All royalties from the sale of this book are being donated to military children's educational causes.

Published simultaneously by Teachers College Press, 1234 Amsterdam Avenue, New York, NY 10027 and by the Military Child Education Coalition®, 909 Mountain Lion Circle, Harker Heights, Texas 76548

Library of Congress Cataloging-in-Publication Data

Astor, Ron Avi, author.
  The military family's parent guide for supporting your child in school / Ron Avi
    Astor, Linda Jacobson, Rami Benbenishty, Julie A. Cederbaum, Hazel Atuel,
    Tamika Gilreath, Marleen Wong, Kris M. Tunac De Pedro, Monica Christina
    Esqueda, and Joey Nuñez Estrada Jr.
      pages cm
  Includes index.
  ISBN 978-0-8077-5368-2 (pbk. : alk. paper)
    1. Children of military personnel–Education–United States–Handbooks,
  manuals, etc. I. Title.
  LC5081.A515 2012
  379.73–dc23   2012020716

ISBN 978-0-8077-5368-2 (paperback)

Printed on acid-free paper
Manufactured in the United States of America

19   18   17   16   15   14   13   12   8   7   6   5   4   3   2   1

Contents

Preface

As we were writing this book, the war in Iraq officially ended, and a date has been set for withdrawing troops from Afghanistan.

Public support for successful reunions between U.S. service members and their families should be strong, so that our men and women in uniform can make smooth transitions to life back at home. Some parents returning from deployments will be looking for new careers in the face of "downsizing," while others will be training for future assignments overseas. These can be stressful times for military families.

Public schools can potentially provide a setting in which children can feel a sense of security. A "bedrock." "A consistent, safe place." Those are the words one principal we talked to used to describe what school should be for children in military families, "no matter what is going on at home, no matter where you are in the deployment cycle."

We have worked with many military-connected school districts in developing this guide. On a regular basis, we heard stories of how resilient military children are—able to quickly adjust to new schools, new friends, and shifting academic demands. And we've witnessed the love and professionalism in these supportive public schools.

But resiliency isn't necessarily an inborn trait. These fantastic schools are fostering strength, courage, and a sense of pride in these students. They honor and celebrate the many layers of sacrifices made by these families. They are making sure a friendly face is there to greet students when they enroll. They are giving them opportunities to talk about the places they have lived. And they are hiring professionals trained to respond during tough times, so children—many of whom have had to take on adult responsibilities in their homes while a parent is away—can focus on being students.

In searching across the country for good ideas, evidence-supported practices, and grassroots efforts, we've learned that school communities can help to relieve some of the stress on military families. Great schools can help military students and families thrive, provide an extra sense of connectedness, and lend a helping hand when needed.

Schools have generated creative ideas to welcome military children. For example, one school created a friendship garden so military children could literally, and figuratively, put down some roots in their new school and feel more connected.

When another school asked military children to serve as "tour guides" and buddies to incoming students, the transition period went much more smoothly and parents felt less anxious about their children's first days in a new place. And others hosted morning coffee chats for military parents so they could get better acquainted and share ideas for supporting each other.

These are simple practices—but they are practices that can be implemented by any school, and that can create positive experiences for children who move an average of nine times before they graduate from high school.

This book was created by a diverse team of professionals at the University of Southern California. Our research included hours of interviews with military families, model school principals, excellent teachers, and military school liaison officers, as well as observations of programs that are working well. We also carefully integrated research, reviewed the literature, searched the Internet, and explored the work of national organizations in selecting the most beneficial practices, programs, and resources to present.

Our deepest hope is that this book provides you with practical and eye-opening ideas for supporting your children through the transitions they will face and for helping your school community better understand your family's challenges and contributions. We hope civilians will recognize that military culture is an important diversity group to include in curriculum and school climate reform. Ultimately, caring, supportive, culturally appropriate, and thoughtful school environments could radically change the lives of all students, but even more so for those who have endured so much.

All of the royalties from the sale of this book are being donated to nonprofit, education-oriented organizations benefitting military children.

Acknowledgments

This guide seeks to make public schools more supportive of military families. We first want to thank the military families who have sacrificed so much for our country. We thank you for your contributions to our society and to our world. Military families and children are strong, proud, and resilient. We saw and heard this every place we went. Many of the ideas generated in this guide originated from educators who themselves had a military family member or who have served. We thank them for their continued commitment.

The authors wish to sincerely thank the many citizens and professionals in school districts, government, the military, and in non-profit organizations who have shared their best practices so we could include them in this guide. We especially want to thank the school liaison officers from all branches of the military who work tirelessly to improve school experiences for military children.

To all the district officials, principals, assistant principals, teachers, pupil personnel, parents, and students: thank you for sharing with us your ideas, stories, and photos so that other schools can learn how to make military children feel more welcome and appreciated. Our partners at San Diego State University, UC San Diego, and the University of California Los Angeles have also been instrumental in elevating this work to a regional level. The over 100 master's and doctoral students in social work and education from USC, as well as the master's students in social work, school counseling, and school psychology from SDSU, also deserve special recognition for inspiring many of the recommendations in this book. We thank the undergraduate students in the Partners at Learning program at UCSD.

Many scientific experts and research organizations have advised us through the process of creating this guide, including the members of our International Advisory Board, various educational consultants, the Military Family Research Institute, the National Military Family Association, and the Department of Defense Education Activity (DoDEA).

In particular, we would like to thank: the DoDEA partnership program for national leadership, excellent materials and programs, and vigilant dissemination of best practices to public schools; the Military Child Education Coalition for educating teachers, counselors, parents, and administrators; the American Association of Colleges of Teacher Education for engaging university schools of education; and most importantly, the University of Southern California (USC) schools of social work and education, the Center for Research and Innovation on Veterans and Military Families, and Hamovitch Research Center for their commitment to train professionals in university settings to work with military families. We also want to recognize Dr. Jill Biden, Michelle Obama, and their staffs for support and for nationally prioritizing the needs of military children and families. Their Joining Forces campaign highlights the need to educate universities and public schools about the needs of military students.

Introduction

> The Pride Club just really had a big impact on me, knowing that she was okay. It reassured me that there are resources out there.
>
> —Monique Felizardo, military spouse, in reference to a club for military children created at her daughter Kayla's school. The club was a supportive place for Kayla following a transfer from Japan to San Diego.

Military children live unique and interesting lives. They have opportunities to travel around the world, to gain firsthand knowledge of cultures that most American students only read about, and can often adapt quickly to new situations and surroundings.

But your children may also face challenges and have special circumstances that civilian children and families don't experience. These can include gaps in school attendance and learning due to frequent moves, being separated from a parent who has been deployed, and a sense of isolation in the midst of a civilian community that cannot relate to the issues and challenges they face.

As a military parent, you may already know that schools vary tremendously in how knowledgeable they are about the military lifestyle and culture and how welcoming they are to incoming families—military or not. Some may have orientation procedures and assign new students a "buddy" or a mentor. They may be very considerate of your family's circumstances. On the other hand, some schools merely check to make sure you have filled out the required forms and allow new students to fend for themselves at lunch, in the hallways, or on the playground.

This variation in approach is something that you will likely encounter as your child ages and as you move from community to community. A lack of attention and sensitivity to your family's military lifestyle may also make you feel as if the teachers and other school personnel don't value the service you or your spouse give to our country.

Realize that most teachers and school principals—unless they were in the military themselves or grew up in a military family—were not trained to recognize how being a military child can impact a student's experiences in school. They are unfamiliar with the cycle of deployment and how it can affect a child's daily life, and may have mistaken assumptions about military families.

This could soon change, however.

The lives of military children are receiving attention at the highest levels of government. A 2011 presidential initiative boosted efforts across all federal agencies to support military families—a focus that is expected to continue in future administrations.

In addition, the Department of Defense and the Department of Education have agreed that supporting military children in civilian schools should be a high priority, and that traditional public, private, and Department of Defense Education Activity (DoDEA) schools should begin sharing information about successful practices and policies. In a letter to superintendents, U.S. Secretary of Education Arne Duncan said, "I ask for your assistance in meeting the needs of military-connected school children. I hope you will help raise awareness with respect to, and provide assistance for, military-connected children and their families in your schools and community." The letter, which you might want to share with your school, is available here: http://www2.ed.gov/policy/gen/guid/secletter/120424. html

All parents want their children to feel welcomed, cared for, and happy when they go off to school in the morning and return in the afternoon. No parent wants to worry that his or her child feels alone, isolated, or frustrated. Schools play an important role in creating friendly, supportive environments in which all students feel valued and connected.

Many military-connected schools–those civilian schools that serve high numbers of military students–are already implementing practices that make transitions and school experiences easier for military students. More schools should learn about these practices and educators should receive training on the unique educational issues faced by military students.

In addition to this guide, we have also written companion versions for pupil personnel (social workers, school counselors, and psychologists), teachers, and school administrators. You can share with staff in your child's school what you have learned from this guide and inform them about the guides that are appropriate for them.

DESCRIPTION OF THIS GUIDE

This guide is intended to give you useful information on researching schools for your child, as well as highlight the kinds of ideas and promising practices that are likely to make military students feel more welcome. In the absence of such efforts in your child's school, we will suggest steps that military parents can take to advocate for their children, with the goal of creating greater awareness among your child's school personnel.

Part of a 4-year project called "Building Capacity to Create Highly Supportive Military-Connected School Districts," this guide is a groundbreaking effort to bridge the gaps between military families and civilian schools and to make those schools more inviting and supportive for this unique group of students.

More specifically, this guide will:

- suggest issues you may want to consider when deciding on the best school for your child. For those of you with young children, this guide will also cover important topics related to child-care and preschool programs;
- highlight a wide variety of organizations, programs, and resources aimed at informing military families about education issues;

- point to publications and initiatives that can help your children through the challenges of growing up in a military household;
- include promising examples of schools and military families working together in the best interests of children.

THE ISSUE OF TRANSITION

As you know, your child will likely change schools much more often than a nonmilitary child. But a school transfer is not the only type of transition your child will encounter. The life of a military child is an ongoing series of transitions that take place even when an actual relocation is not involved. This is important to keep in mind and is a theme that will cut across all topics addressed in this guide.

Every time you or your spouse is deployed or returns from an assignment is a transition that can lead to changing roles in your family's structure and routine or changing relationships with your children.

Simply being "the new kid" in school is not the only time your child may become preoccupied with the multitude of events and changes occurring within their immediate environment. It's important that schools become a source of ongoing support and stability during these times.

"[Children] need something that they can rely on that's consistent, especially with multiple deployments," says Diana Ashe, a mother, a former Marine, and the wife of a Marine. She also holds a Master's of Social Work from USC. "The more constant structure you can have within a school and everybody working within a community and as a group, the better off the kids will be."

It is our hope that this guide contributes to helping parents find schools that are more welcoming, accommodating, and sensitive to children growing up in a military home.

Please note that the web links we have provided throughout this guide are as up-to-date as possible. But we know that websites change and links sometimes disappear. Please search the Internet for the resource if our link doesn't work.

A Note to Parent Leaders

If you serve in a leadership role in your school, think of ways your parent organization can support military families. Here are a few ideas:

- Hold a resource fair at the beginning of the school year in which you invite military and community-based organizations to bring information about their services.
- Organize an activity in which students make care packages or holiday cards for soldiers on deployment.
- Invite school liaison officers to the school for an informational session on how they can assist military families.
- Offer to organize play dates or carpools for families in which one parent is deployed.
- When a student moves away—even if they are not from a military family—prepare a special gift for the student to take with them. Ideas might include a memory book with photos and notes from classmates, a school T-shirt signed by classmates, a framed photo, or even a stuffed animal that is the mascot of the school.
- On Memorial Day or Veterans Day, invite a military parent to a school assembly or to say the Pledge of Allegiance that day.

CHAPTER 1

Mobility

Military families often prefer living among or near other military families–either on or off base–because they find it easier to associate with other parents and children who share similar lifestyles. But don't let your choice of neighbors be the only factor you consider in preparation for a move.

The school your child will attend can also play a large part in whether he or she has a smooth transition following the move. Will the school offer a welcoming environment as well as programs and services designed to assist your child both academically and socially? Or will the school place all the burdens on the parents and the child if the child is struggling to overcome learning gaps or emotional problems? These are questions to think about before selecting your child's school.

Decision Point:
Is This Move Right for Your Family?

Are you moving because you received Permanent Change of Station orders? Or are you moving to be closer to friends and family during a deployment? If this move is not an official transfer, are you considering how it will affect your child's progress in school? Are you exploring options for completing the school year instead of moving in the middle of the year?

If you must move, gather as much information ahead of time about the school your child will attend, and make contact by phone or email with a counselor or office staff person so you have someone to connect with when you and your child arrive.

**Decision Point:
High Test Scores or Military Friendly?**

What are your highest priorities in choosing a school for your child? Do you want them to be around other military children, or is it more important that they are in a school where students are scoring above district and state averages and most students are on track to go to college?

Ideally, the school your child attends will be both high achieving and welcoming to military families, but it's possible that you will have to make compromises in order to find a school that meets your child's needs.

In this chapter on Mobility, you will find information on both choosing a school as well as issues that you will want to consider as your child makes the transition.

HOW CAN CHANGING SCHOOLS AFFECT YOUR CHILD?

Every child reacts differently to being the "new kid." Some pick up right where they left off at their previous school, while others struggle to adapt either socially or academically. Even if your child has not previously changed schools or hasn't had any trouble in the past, it's important that you understand the primary issues that can create challenges for your children.

Inconsistent academic standards: When your child enters a new school, it's possible that he or she has not learned some of the material that the new school has already covered earlier in the year. But it's also just as likely that he or she has already mastered a skill or topic that the school has not yet introduced.

This is because there is wide variation across states in what students are expected to know and when they are expected to know it. This mismatch between schools becomes even more critical as children enter high school and begin accumulating credits for graduation. If courses or exams taken in one state are not accepted in another, the student may not meet the requirements for graduation—even though they were on track in the last school they attended.

Extracurricular activities: If your child plays sports or participates in other extracurricular activities, such as drama, chorus, or academic teams, it's possible that he or she will miss out on the chance to stay in these activities when your family relocates because of missed tryouts or auditions, or because your child does not meet eligibility criteria in the new school. Talk to school administrators about whether they can waive certain requirements or accept letters of recommendation from previous coaches or teachers as long as your child is qualified.

Special education: If your child has special needs, relocation can create a variety of challenges. Just because your child had an individualized education program or a 504 plan in his or her previous school does not mean the same services will automatically be available in the new school. On the other hand, it's also possible that a child was labeled as a special education student in the last school because of problems related to being a military child or is referred to special education in the new school for no good reason. You may already be familiar with the Exceptional Family Member Program, which is intended to make sure the individual's medical, emotional, and behavioral needs are met when a military member on active duty is transferred. Special education services vary, however, across civilian school districts. See our expanded section on Students with Special Needs in Chapter 2.

Parental involvement: Just because you or your spouse is in the military does not mean that you can't be involved in your child's education. In fact, surveys show that military parents are often very involved in school activities and support their children's education at home. You might need to work with your school, however, to gain flexibility regarding parent-teacher conferences or volunteer opportunities—especially when a parent is deployed.

Social adjustment: A child who moves frequently may feel that he or she doesn't want to go to the trouble of making new friends again. Military students report that wondering where they will fit in and who they will eat lunch with can create tremendous stress. If you see evidence of this, talk to a teacher or counselor about your concerns.

HOW SHOULD YOU CHOOSE A SCHOOL?

Once your orders are received, it is best to do some research on the schools and school districts near the installation where you are headed.

A variety of resources provide information on schools in the community where you are transferring. Some websites are targeted specifically to military parents, while others are aimed at a broader audience.

Be careful, however, not to limit your background search to one source. Consult multiple sources in order to gather the most accurate picture of the schools available to you.

ONLINE TOOLS

Great Schools, www.greatschools.org: This free service ranks schools on a scale from 1 to 10, with 10 being the best. The ratings are based on recent standardized test results in each state. Results usually reflect the percentage of students scoring at or above the proficient level on the test in each grade and subject. While test scores are not the only measurement that should be used to choose a school, they are a strong indicator of the academic success of the school.

You can also view the Great Schools information by subgroup category to determine, for example, how English learners are performing at the school their children might be attending. In addition, the site features parent comments, which can provide some insight into what members of the community think about the school. But realize that these comments have not been verified and should not be used as the only source to make your decision regarding school attendance.

Information is also available on the school district that the school is part of, so parents can view the rankings for all the schools in the district. But also understand that sometimes the information is not up to date.

School Quest, http://www.schoolquest.org: This website is an initiative of the Military Child Education Coalition (MCEC), so it is especially geared toward military families.

In addition to a school search function, the site offers articles and MCEC's "Ask Aunt Peggie" feature for posing questions regarding school records, transferring credits, or other issues you might be wondering about. "Aunt Peggie" is an expert researcher for the MCEC and serves as a resource for families and educators around the world. She is a former military-connected child who attended nine schools by 12th grade. Her 34 years of experience in school administration and the classroom makes her well qualified to respond to the concerns of military families. She can be reached by e-mail at peggie.watson@militarychild.org.

ACCOUNTABILITY DATA

States and the federal government set goals for student achievement at each school. As a result, there is a wealth of official government data available on individual schools. Most schools are issued a "report card" by their state, which includes student test score data, and can also include school safety reports, teacher certification information, and other categories.

Many school districts also collect and distribute their own monitoring or progress reports on their schools. These reports are helpful for getting a sense of what priorities and goals schools have set for themselves and what they are doing to reach those targets.

At the federal level, the No Child Left Behind Act (NCLB), also known as the Elementary and Secondary Education Act (ESEA), sets specific achievement goals for schools to meet. If your children have previously attended DoDEA schools, this system is similar to

DoDEA's School Report Cards, which includes demographic data on schools as well as test scores.

Under NCLB, schools are accountable for making "adequate yearly progress" (AYP) in student achievement, including the subgroups of students that they serve, such as African Americans or children with disabilities. Schools that miss those performance targets must enter a process of improving their programs. Schools that don't make AYP for multiple years can face more serious consequences. With ESEA currently up for reauthorization by Congress, there could be significant changes to this accountability system in the coming years. One of the changes for which our team advocates is that military students be considered as a special cultural group and that performance goals for these students be consistently monitored. The education agency in each state provides information on AYP results for all districts and schools. In addition to Great Schools, an AYP report is another source to consult in gathering knowledge about the school your child might attend.

OTHER RESOURCES

State education resources: This section of the School Quest site provides information on topics such as states' academic standards, testing requirements and schedules, gifted and talented programs, charter schools, and online learning programs. http://www.schoolquest.org/state-education-resources/

Education Commission of the States: This organization's website includes information on each state's kindergarten laws, including entrance age. http://www.ecs.org/html/issueEL_new.asp

The military parent's guide to No Child Left Behind: MCEC provides this booklet to familiarize military parents with the federal education law and how it can affect and benefit their child. The booklet can be ordered through the online store for $3.50. http://militarychild.org

Helping military children get a good public education may require that we view them as members of a distinct American cultural group. Military families readily agree they make up a subculture with its own history, rituals, values, music, and experiences. Department of Defense schools on bases accommodate this culture in their curriculum and support networks.

—Dr. Ron Astor, Building Capacity project leader, on making military children a unique subgroup as part of No Child Left Behind

Students at the Center: This guide from DoDEA's Military K–12 Partners website speaks to the various groups involved in helping military students be successful: parents, civilian school officials, and military leaders. The family section provides information on a military child's unique needs, the advocacy role of parents, and navigating the U.S. education system. http://www.militaryk12partners. dodea.edu/studentsAtTheCenter/index.html

Central Union School District's Transition Specialist

When military families arrive in the Central Union School District near Fresno, California—the site of Naval Air Station Lemoore— they don't have to feel lost or left with questions over how to help their children adjust to their new school.

Anne Gonzales, the district's transition specialist, is there to welcome new students and their parents, monitor their adjustment in the new school, and respond to any ongoing issues the students are having either academically, socially, or emotionally. Most of her work takes place in the district's two "base" schools, Akers Elementary and Neutra Elementary. Gonzales, a vice-principal at Akers, also has a background as a school social worker.

"Students are coming from everywhere and they come from many, many different special circumstances and stressors," says Gonzales. "We do see the need for addressing transition."

Transition Specialist Anne Gonzales, top right, meets with parent Christa Carlson and her daughters Trinity, bottom right, and Riley at Akers Elementary on Naval Air Station Lemoore in California. The family arrived during the school year.

Photo by
Mary Lawson

Gonzales meets with new students and their parents—sometimes even on the day they come in to register. She has to assure them that when they are called to her office that it is not because they are in trouble. She will review transcripts—especially those of middle grade students—to see if there are any gaps in their schooling, and talk to the students about whether they understand what is being taught in their new classes, and whether they are making friends.

While most of the 1,300 students at the two schools live in housing on the base, some live in surrounding neighborhoods, which can also affect their peer group and what they are doing after school.

New students are part of her "caseload" for 3 months, but if a student demonstrates a need for ongoing support, she remains involved.

On a typical day, Gonzales meets with eight to ten students, and might also talk with the same number of parents. She also participates in individualized education program (IEP) meetings and works with teachers to discuss ways to differentiate instruction for students.

THE INTERSTATE COMPACT ON EDUCATIONAL
OPPORTUNITY FOR MILITARY CHILDREN

As a military parent, it is important for you to know about the efforts of many states to make school changes simpler for military students.

Growing up in a military family, your children are likely to change schools almost every 3 years, the consequences of which vary depending on their age and grade level. For example, at the kindergarten level, your child could begin the school year in one state, where the enrollment guidelines allow a student to enter kindergarten just after turning 5. But you and your family might transfer mid-year to a school in a state with a much earlier cut-off date—suddenly making your child too young for kindergarten.

In the early grades, differences in state policy, while problematic, are to a degree benign. But as your children get older, the stakes associated with these differences become higher and can produce dire consequences. For example, to earn a high school diploma, many states require that graduating seniors complete a course in state history (e.g., California state history in California). If your child begins school in one state and transfers to a high school in a different state, it can be difficult to fulfill that requirement in time for graduation, a reality that can stand in the way of your child's postsecondary opportunities.

Prior to April 2008, states lacked a uniform policy to address the needs of military children in transition. Issues related to enrollment, course/program placement, eligibility and graduation were generally addressed on a case-by-case basis. While the Department of Defense had long worked with individual school districts, primarily those with high military enrollments, to reduce the difficulties associated with student transition, stakeholders and policymakers agreed that much more could and needed to be done at both the state and local level. They hoped that once enacted, an interstate compact—a contractual agreement entered into by two or more states in areas that are traditionally protected by state sovereignty (e.g., on education policy)—would supersede conflicting state laws related to the transition of military children from school to school and across state lines.

The Interstate Compact on Educational Opportunity for Military Children is designed to facilitate or provide for:

- the timely enrollment of children [from] military families and [ensure] that they are not placed at a disadvantage due to difficulty in the transfer of education records between schools or variations in entrance/age requirements
- the student placement process through which children of military families are not disadvantaged by variations in attendance requirements, scheduling, sequencing, grading, course content, or assessment
- the qualification and eligibility for enrollment, educational programs, and participation in extracurricular academic, athletic, and social activities
- the on-time graduation of children of military families
- promulgation and enforcement of administrative rules implementing the provisions of [the] compact
- for the uniform collection and sharing of information between and among member states, schools, and military families under [the] compact
- coordination between this compact and other compacts affecting military children
- flexibility and coordination between the educational system, parents, and the student in order to achieve educational success for the student

Source: Council of State Governments. (2008). *Interstate compact on educational opportunity for military children: Legislative resource kit.* Available at http://www.csg.org/programs/policyprograms/NCIC/MIC3ResourcesandPublications.aspx.

The purpose of the Interstate Compact on Educational Opportunity for Military Children is to reduce and/or eliminate "barriers to educational success" for children from military families as they transition between schools and across state lines.

The compact also provides for the creation of individual state councils and an interstate commission. According to the Council of

State Governments, unless otherwise specified, the Interstate Compact applies to the children of:

- active duty military personnel
- members of the uniformed services, including the four main branches as well as the Commissioned Corps of the National Oceanic and Atmospheric Administration, and Public Health Services
- veterans of the uniformed services who are "medically discharged or retired" up to "one year after medical discharge or retirement"
- "members of the uniformed services who" are deceased as a result of their service within the past year

As of this writing, 42 states have endorsed the Interstate Compact. While the responsiveness of states to the compact is a positive development, implementing it at the local level has been challenging–something you may have experienced. An organizational structure, however, is emerging and continues to evolve. Despite having endorsed this legislation, some states have done so only symbolically and have not informed district superintendents and/or school personnel of the compact's policy implications. In the absence of state action, however, some districts have begun to implement their own policies to ease the transition of military children.

Broadly conceived, the goal of the Interstate Compact is to provide systemic support to military children in the areas that have historically been problematic–enrollment, course or program placement, eligibility, and graduation. Gaps in the dissemination of information and implementation, however, hinder the ability of civilian public schools to provide consistent support to military children. Moving forward, greater awareness and understanding of the compact is needed. You can assist in this process by becoming familiar with the compact, sharing the information with school officials, and asking for district policies that help military students. For more information on the Interstate Compact, visit www.mic3.net.

Please note, the following article correction: The compact *does* include policies addressing high school exit exams. Check with your state and/or school district regarding its policy as states have taken different approaches to the issue.

The above material is an excerpt from Esqueda, M. C., Astor, R. A., & De Pedro, K. (2012). A call to duty: Educational policy and school reform addressing the needs of children from military families. *Educational Researcher, 41*(2), 65–70.

KNOW YOUR LIAISON

Even before enrolling your child in a new school, it's important to be aware that as a military family, you have someone who can inform you and advocate for you and your child regarding educational issues. This person is a school liaison, and each branch of the military has liaison officers who can serve as a connection between the military and the public schools. Many of these specialists have either served in the military, are a military spouse, and/or have a background in education.

Their mission is to address any education-related problems or barriers that might keep your child from having a positive experience. In the Marines, they are called school liaisons and for the Air Force, they are called "point-of-contact" advocates. These officers are often based on military installations, but in some cases, their offices are actually housed as part of the local school district to improve communication and cooperation with school officials and staff. You can find a director of liaison officers on the Military K–12 Partners website at http://www.militaryk12partners.dodea.edu/index.cfm.

WHAT QUESTIONS SHOULD YOU ASK
BEFORE YOUR CHILD ENTERS A NEW SCHOOL?

Even with the Interstate Compact, you may still have many pressing concerns about your own child's transition into a new school. This list may only cover a few of those issues. But how schools answer these

**Decision Point:
Should You Tell the School
That You Are a Military Family?**

Perhaps because you have felt misunderstood or even discriminated against in the past—and you don't want your child to experience this—you may be inclined to keep your military status private. But awareness of the needs of military students among educators won't increase if someone doesn't present them with the issues. They can't be supportive if they don't know.

may give you a glimpse into the learning and social climate they have created for students. This section also covers topics that apply to children of *any age*–K–12. Later in this chapter, we also offer suggestions for families with preschoolers and issues to consider if you have a child in high school.

Can we have a tour? Visiting the new school with your child and meeting a few key teachers and students before your child's first day in the classroom might make your son or daughter far more comfortable in their new surroundings. It's possible that the school might offer this opportunity or even have a routine procedure for introducing new students to the school. But if they don't, you can make this suggestion.

The public schools, where it's integrated with civilian and Marine Corps kids, they don't really know. The most they know about the Marine Corps is like that they shoot stuff. They kinda don't really know what you're going through. They try to sympathize with you but it's not really the same. They're great friends and everything but they just don't understand what you're going through. The military kids are really accepting. It's really easy to just fit right in because they all know what you're going through. They all move around a lot.

—Koah Patton, 14

Can we meet the teachers? If your tour doesn't include a visit with your child's teacher or teachers, ask for a brief introduction and a few minutes to get to know each other. Meeting their teacher(s) might also make your children feel less nervous and can give them a chance to tell their teacher something about themselves, such as their favorite subjects or what they enjoyed about their most recent school. If your child is in middle or high school, there will be multiple teachers and you might instead want to request a meeting with just one, such as the homeroom teacher, or a language arts teacher.

Can we talk to a counselor? If your new school has a counselor, psychologist, or social worker (often called "pupil personnel"), this person might be an important contact to have as your child adjusts to the new school—especially if you think your child might have trouble making friends or keeping up with schoolwork. You can request a meeting alone or include your child. These professionals are aware of any concerns you might have over protecting your child's privacy.

How many of your students are from military families? And do you have any particular services or programs geared toward these students? If the school is on a base, chances are military students represent close to 100% of the student enrollment. But if the school is located in the surrounding community, the school may or may not know how many military students they have. If they can provide you with an approximate figure, this could indicate that the leadership recognizes that military students are part of their community and that the school may even have services or programs geared toward military children. If someone at the school doesn't offer to introduce you to other military parents, don't be hesitant to ask.

How stable is the staff? If there has been a lot of turnover in both the teaching and administrative ranks at the school, this might just be coincidence or it could indicate that there are reasons the staff doesn't want to stay. It's likely that the school—and maybe even the district—will tell you that they don't have this information, so it is something you might have to glean from outside sources.

Does your school have any former military or current Reserve or National Guard members? Making a connection at the school with someone who understands the challenges facing military parents and students might make you and your child feel more comfortable during the first few weeks.

What opportunities do you have for parent involvement? If the answer is only "We have a parent organization," this could indicate that the school hasn't thought very creatively about how to reach out to parents or to include them in their child's education. See the box

---

Six Types of Parent Involvement

According to the National Network of Partnership Schools at Johns Hopkins University, there are six different forms of parent involvement. Each one of these should be viewed with military families in mind.

- **Parenting:** Assisting families with parenting skills and setting home conditions to support children as students. Also, assisting schools to better understand families—in this case, military families.
- **Communicating:** Conducting effective communications from school to home and from home to school about programs and student progress.
- **Volunteering:** Organizing volunteers and audiences to support the school and students. Providing volunteer opportunities in various locations and at various times.
- **Learning at Home:** Involving families with their children on homework and other curriculum-related activities and decisions.
- **Decisionmaking:** Involving families as participants in school decisions and developing parent leaders and representatives.
- **Collaborating with the Community:** Coordinating resources and services from the community for families, students, and the school and providing services to the community.

on the Six Types of Parent Involvement from the National Network of Partnership Schools at Johns Hopkins University.

As a military parent, there also may be times that you won't be able to participate in school-related activities at the same level as you would like. When talking with school leaders or teachers, ask about alternatives to traditional volunteer opportunities. Also, ask about how deployed parents can remain involved with what is happening at school.

In addition to viewing any information from the PTA or PTO, look at other outside groups that support the schools, such as a Local Education Fund, to get a sense of what is happening in the district.

How do you and your teachers communicate with parents? Ask about the various methods that teachers will use to communicate with you about school activities and your child's performance. Can you e-mail them if you have questions? Do teachers have web pages that list homework assignments or other important information? Is there an online service you can use to track grades and assignments being completed? The more information you have about what is expected of students, the better you can support your child's progress.

WHAT ARE YOUR CHILD'S NEEDS?

As you make the transition into the new school, think ahead about how your child is faring academically, socially, and emotionally. This will help you articulate to new teachers or counselors how they can best support your child. And if the school can't meet the need, you'll know what you need to look for in the community.

Will your child be out of step academically with other students? After your child starts the new school, you'll most likely be able to tell whether he or she is on pace with the curriculum in this new state and district. If your child's grades are suddenly declining compared with grades in previous schools, then it may be possible that your child is missing some material that these students have already learned. Ask the school whether tutoring services are available to help your child catch up. If not, ask them for recommendations on tutoring help in the community.

In addition, there are some online tutoring services designed specifically for military students.

- Tutor.com, www.tutor.com/military, provides free tutoring for military families.
- Another service, Student Online Achievement Resources, www.soarathome.com, offers assessments linked to state standards as well as lessons to review and teach skills that students might lack.

On the other hand, your child might complain that his or her classes are repeating material that he or she has already studied. In this case, you might ask the teacher or teachers whether your child can work ahead independently or complete some extra enrichment activities. Is it possible for the child to join students in the next grade for the particular subject where they are advanced?

If you have a high school student who is now acquiring credits for graduation, the issue of mobility is even more critical. If possible, meet or talk by phone with a counselor at the new school even before your child enrolls to discuss courses your child has already completed and how they compare to expectations in the new school. If courses on the transcript are similar in content, but don't match exactly, can waivers be granted? May your child take an online course to receive needed credit? Refer back to the section on the Interstate Compact on Educational Opportunity for Military Children.

March2Success, www.march2success.com/index.cfm, is another online service that provides practice for students in the areas of SAT or ACT preparation and state standardized tests. There is also a section focusing on college admissions and financing.

What sports or extracurricular activities does your child participate in or enjoy? While it's certainly important that your child avoid roadblocks in their academic progress when they change schools, making sure they continue to do what they enjoy outside of class will assist them in forming new friendships and can provide them with a distraction during stressful times.

Ask the school what sports and other extracurricular activities and clubs they offer. If the school your child will be attending doesn't have something that he or she was enjoying at their previous school, they might be willing to try something new, or you might want to search for community-based programs through Parks and Recreations departments to fill the need.

If your state has adopted the Interstate Compact on the Education of Military Children, your new school should also be following guidelines regarding eligibility for sports or other extracurricular activities that allow your child to participate without having to pass additional tryouts or auditions. See our special section on the Compact earlier in this chapter.

Does your child have an IEP? If your child has a special need, you will have another layer of issues to consider when your child starts a new school. See our section in Chapter 2 on Special Education.

Is your child still learning English? Schools have a variety of models for teaching children to become proficient in English. Bilingual education, immersion, two-way immersion, and structured English immersion are some of the terms you might hear in reference to the school's approach toward English language development. If the school doesn't ask about your child's literacy skills in English, or doesn't provide a short assessment to evaluate their skills, make sure you bring up this topic if your child is still developing his or her English fluency.

Was this most recent move especially difficult? Does your child struggle to make new friends? Does he or she have trouble asking for help? Even an outgoing child can feel shy in a new place. And even if they seemed to handle previous moves with little trouble, perhaps this move meant leaving the best teacher they've ever had or a first boyfriend or girlfriend. Don't make generalizations about your child's behavior and disposition based on past moves. They have changed since then. If the school hasn't offered to assign your child a "buddy" for the first few days of school, ask a teacher to see that this happens.

Will your child need before- or after-school programs and care? Some schools have on-site before- and after-school programs, although they usually aren't free. If the school doesn't provide any extended care, ask if they have partnerships with outside agencies such as the YMCA, a Parks and Recreation Department, or the Boys and Girls Clubs. Some of these providers will also offer transportation between the school and the program.

The Afterschool Alliance, http://www.afterschoolalliance.org/index.cfm, is a national organization that provides advice on how to search for after-school programs as well as information about providers and activities in each state.

WHAT ELSE CAN YOU DO TO HELP
YOUR CHILD MAKE A SMOOTH TRANSITION?

Ask for an exit interview: If your current school doesn't offer a spring or end-of-the-year parent-teacher conference, ask for a meeting to gain as much information as possible about where your child stands academically. Even if a year-end conference is planned, you might miss this because not all moves for military families are conveniently aligned with the academic calendar. Your child's current teachers or counselor can recommend specific skills your child may need to work on as he or she heads to a new school and may suggest certain websites or workbooks for extra help. They may be willing to provide this information in detail and in writing, so that you could share it with staff in the new school. They might even agree to call the new school to talk about any learning issues or special talents your child might have. You can help by having the phone number and even a contact person's name available to them.

Letters of recommendation: Some parents have found it useful to ask for letters of recommendation from current teachers to take with them to the new school. While this may seem more appropriate for a child preparing for college, even an elementary teacher can benefit from reading what the child's previous teacher has to say about his or her strengths and weaknesses. You want your child's new school to recognize your son or daughter as an individual and to focus on their specific needs, interests, and strengths. A letter from your child's teacher can help accomplish this.

Photo book: Younger children might appreciate a small photo album or book that includes pictures of their new school. This might require cooperation from a secretary at the new school in order to obtain some pictures of the child's new teacher, a typical classroom, or the playground. Or if you know another military family that is already stationed in that community, you can ask for their assistance in taking some pictures of the outside of the building. This makes the experience less of an unknown for the child. You could use a commercial service such as Shutterfly to make a book, but you can also pick up a simple empty photo album to insert some pictures.

Visit the school's website: The new school's website might have a photo gallery, a letter from the principal, links to web pages of teachers for your child's grade level, and other visual features that can give both you and your child an indication of what students are currently studying, special activities held at the school, and opportunities to get involved. Staff e-mail addresses, if listed, can also give you and your child an opportunity to connect with someone before you arrive.

Facebook: As a parent, you may still have reservations about allowing your child to use social media. But many teens are now far more likely to communicate via Facebook, by text, or through another social media site than by email or phone. Safeguards do exist, and using social media will allow your older children to remain in closer contact with friends they have made around the country and around the world. During those initial uncomfortable weeks in a new place—or if your child continues to feel alone in their new school—staying in touch online may be a way for them to receive ongoing support and friendship. Many schools also have Facebook pages, which can provide your child another way to learn about the new school.

Talk to your school liaison: Your military school liaison in the current school or district could be helpful in connecting you with military educational resources in your new community. A military liaison there may have important insights and tips for you as you make decisions and prepare your family for the move to a new school and community.

OTHER RESOURCES

A variety of resources, websites, and programs exist to support military families and children when they move. Some sites include information on transferring into new schools. Here are a few you may already know about and some you may not:

National Military Family Association, http://www.militaryfamily.org/: Publications from this organization include the "We Serve, Too" toolkits—one about younger children and one about teens. Both discuss ways to support military children and offer specific examples of practices or strategies that schools or other organizations can use to foster a sense of pride and belonging in military children as well as help them through transitions, separation, and war.

Military One Source, http://www.militaryonesource.com/default.aspx: As its name implies, this website aims to be a one-stop shop for information, advice, and support for military members and their families. There are phone numbers listed to reach a consultant as well as links to articles. Registration is required to gain full access to the materials.

National Guard Bureau Joint Services Support, http://www. jointservicessupport.org/Default.aspx: This site has information and links to resources organized by state. It includes resources for Guard families and children.

Military.com, http://www.military.com/, is a comprehensive site that covers almost every subject you might have questions about, including moving. There are also online networks of military spouses and articles focusing on military children.

Blue Star Families, http://www.bluestarfam.org/: Founded in 2008, this organization strives to be both a voice for military families through its regular surveys as well as a provider of programs and discounts. Chapters exist throughout the country. An online membership community also exists on Facebook.

Moms Over Miles, http://www.momsovermiles.com/, is a website designed to support moms who have to be separated from their children, including military moms. In your family, maybe the mother is the deployed service member, or perhaps the mother has to be separated from the children in the midst of the moving process. This site offers ideas for activities that can help keep mothers and their children connected when they are not physically together.

A companion site for fathers is called **Dads at a Distance**. http:// www.fambooks.com/daads.htm

Military Community Youth Ministries, http://www.mcym.org/, is a Christian organization designed to support military adolescents in middle and high school. Its "Club Beyond" program exists at 19 bases across the United States and at more than 20 in Europe, offering service projects, retreats, summer camps, and weekly meetings.

Our Military Kids, http://www.ourmilitarykids.org/, is an organization that provides support in the form of grants to the children of National Guard and Military Reserve personnel who are currently deployed overseas, as well as the children of wounded warriors in all branches.

RESOURCES FOR YOUR CHILD

Journals, picture books, photo albums, organizers, and other resources that speak directly to military children can help your son or daughter understand that other children and teens have felt the same way they do and can offer suggestions on how to cope with the ongoing changes in their lives.

"My Life as I Move" is one of three journals from the Health Net Federal Services' children's initiative. The journal is designed to help children hold on to memories from the places they have lived and recognize the special people they have met along the way. https://www.hnfs.net/content/hnfs/home/tn/bene/res/symbolic_links/kids_journals.html

Military Youth on the Move is a website directed to children that talks about the challenges of leaving schools and friends behind and adjusting to new places. Other topics such as deployment, divorce, and just regular topics for kids, such as opening a bank account or getting a summer job, are also covered. There are separate sections for elementary, middle, and high school students. http://apps.mhf.dod.mil/pls/psgprod/f?p=MYOM:HOME:0

USO Treehouse is a page on the USO website that offers games and activities for military children. http://www.uso.org/uso-treehouse.aspx

WHAT IF YOU HAVE PRESCHOOL CHILDREN?

The learning experiences that children have during their early years have been found to have a significant impact on their later performance in school. When children attend nurturing child-care and preschool programs with well-planned activities and opportunities for rich vocabulary development, they are more likely to start kindergarten well prepared for the academic expectations in school than if they spent those years in care that only attended to their basic needs.

Even if your children are not in public school yet, there are still issues to consider when exploring early learning options in the community where you are moving.

What Should You Know About the Military System?

You might be familiar with the military child-care system, which is considered a high-quality network of child development centers, family child-care homes, and programs for school-age children. The system provides care for over 200,000 children at over 300 locations worldwide, and has served as a model for civilian programs to follow in areas such as having uniform standards, earning accreditation from a national professional organization, and establishing a compensation system for staff that rewards them for increased training and experience.

The MilitaryHOMEFRONT website provides an overview of the military child-care system and how it operates. http://www.militaryhomefront.dod.mil/portal/page/mhf/MHF/MHF_HOME_1?section_id=20.40.500.94.0.0.0.0.0

A recent survey from the Pew Center on the States (see link on page 32), however, showed that many military families still lack access to these programs. The survey showed that military families are concerned about finding quality child-care and preschool programs—including temporary and drop-in programs during times of increased stress—even more than they are with health care.

The respondents—500 active duty, National Guard and Reserve members—said they value the quality of military child development centers located on base. But many parents, particularly National Guard members and Reservists who don't live on base, still don't have access to these programs.

What If Your Child Stays Home?

Even if your young child does not attend a child-care or preschool program, there are a variety of things you can do to keep your child learning and to prepare him or her for entering kindergarten.

- *Read every day.* Nothing builds language skills, encourages imagination, and contributes to general knowledge about the world like reading. Seek out free story times at local libraries and bookstores to give children group interaction.
- *Maintain your home language.* If your child doesn't know English yet, don't stop reading or speaking to him or her in your family's native language. Strong vocabulary and literacy skills in a child's home language can contribute to quicker mastery of English.
- *Point out patterns.* Recognizing patterns in everyday life builds math skills. Count and sort items with your child at home by size, color, texture, etc.
- *Use the web.* PBS.com and other educational sites have games that teach rhyming words, letter sounds, and other early literacy skills.
- *Join or form a playgroup.* Parents can rotate the task of planning an activity or an outing for the day.
- *Visit your future school.* If you know where your child will attend pre-K or kindergarten, visit and ask for a tour even before the official orientation is scheduled. Make it a familiar place for your child.

   Resources: Here are a few sites that suggest learning activities that can be done at home.

- **Scholastic's** parent site http://www.scholastic.com/parents/
- **Sesame Street's** parent page http://www.sesamestreet.org/parents
- **Zero to Three**. This is a policy and advocacy site, but it offers some important information on infant and toddler development. The organization also has a special section of its website devoted to military families. http://www.zerotothree.org/

The report, "On the Home Front: Early Care and Education a Top Priority for Military Families" recommended an increase in infant and toddler care, greater access to state-funded prekindergarten programs, and using Impact Aid funds allocated to military-connected school districts for early learning programs. Visit this link to read the report: http://www.pewstates.org/uploadedFiles/PCS_Assets/2011/ PEW_PkN_2011_MilitaryFamiliesSurvey.pdf

How Can You Recognize Quality Early Childhood Education Programs?

Whether out of necessity or preference, you may be searching for an early childhood program that is not affiliated with the military. The landscape of programs in the United States can be a confusing mix of centers and home-based programs. Most parents pay the entire cost of child-care and preschool programs, while some qualify for subsidized care based on their income.

Choosing the best place for your child can be a daunting task. You will likely seek the advice of friends or co-workers in the area, but there are also some resources available to help guide you in the process. Child Care Aware of America (CCAA, formerly the National Association of Child Care Resource and Referral Agencies, NAC-CRRA) in Washington, D.C., lists five components of programs to consider:

Adult-to-child ratio: How many children are cared for by each adult? The younger the child, the more important it is for them to receive more individual attention. For babies, experts recommend no more than four babies for one adult caregiver. But by the time children are 4, most do well in a group of 10 with one teacher.

Group size: The size of the group also matters. CCAA describes it this way: "Imagine a group of 25 two-year-olds with five adults, compared to a group of 10 with two adults. Both groups have the same adult to child ratio. Which would be calmer and safer? Which would be more like a family?"

Caregiver/teacher qualifications: What kind of training and education does the child-care provider, or teacher, have to work with young children? Those with two- or four-year degrees and/or special training will be more likely to understand children's needs and help them learn. Do the providers participate in ongoing training to learn about new teaching strategies and research?

Staff turnover: Young children need to form secure attachments to the adults who care for them, including child-care providers and preschool teachers. It is in these relationships that they are more likely to learn and explore their surroundings. When choosing an early-childhood program, ask about the staff turnover rate. Have teachers worked there a long time? Growing up in a military family, your child will experience a lot of changes in his or her life. But that is why it is even more important that you and your child have caregivers that you can count on while you are in your current location.

Accreditation: Ask whether the program you are considering has been accredited by a national organization. Accredited programs must meet standards for their classrooms and services that are higher than what most state licensing agencies require. The National Association for the Education of Young Children (NAEYC), for center-based programs, and the National Association for Family Child Care (NAFCC), for home-based programs, are the two largest accrediting organizations.

How Can You Find a Child-Care or Preschool Program?

Child-care resource and referral agencies (R&Rs), located in every state, help families find early-childhood programs in their area. Depending on your location, there are also R&Rs that focus on particular metro regions.

Recognizing the unique challenges and frequent moves that military families face, Child Care Aware of America has formed a partnership with the four branches of the military to assist families in finding care. Its website provides links to information about eligibility criteria

---

Quality Rating and Improvement Systems (QRIS)

Many states now rate child-care and other early learning programs in order to give parents a guide to follow when they are searching for programs. These systems are in some ways comparable to the grades health departments give restaurants so customers will know where to eat.

Early-childhood programs with higher ratings—more stars, for example—have met higher standards for teacher qualifications, staff-child ratios, and other measures of quality.

See if your state has a QRIS system by visiting the QRIS National Learning Network. Click on State Resources and Profiles. http://qrisnetwork.org/

---

for off-base subsidized child-care programs for the four branches of the military, as well as phone numbers of centers. For more information, visit http://www.naccrra.org/military-families.

What Else Should You Know About Preschool?

As children approach 3 and 4 years old, they are usually ready for more organized learning activities that might not be available in a child-care center or family child-care home. At this stage, many parents start thinking about their child's knowledge of pre-academic skills such as letter sounds, counting, shapes, and colors. Being able to complete a task, pay attention to a teacher, and follow simple instructions are also classroom skills that help children to be ready for school.

As with child-care programs, there are both public preschool programs supported by state or local funds, as well as private programs that parents pay for themselves. In general, you will want to ask the same questions about ratio, group size, teacher qualifications, turnover, and accreditation when looking at preschool programs. There are also varying philosophies among educators and parents regarding how children should spend their time in preschool, with some being more play-oriented and others leaning more toward structured lessons.

Over the past 15 years, state legislatures have significantly increased efforts to make public preschool programs available to more families. More than 40 states now have state-funded preschool programs, although most of them limit enrollment to low-income families. Some refer to their programs as pre-kindergarten because they are only open to 4-year-olds in the year before they attend kindergarten.

A few states, including Oklahoma, Florida, and Georgia, operate "universal" pre-K programs, meaning that any 4-year-old—regardless of how much their parents earn—is eligible to attend.

In recent years, some states have also adjusted their eligibility rules to make sure that children of military families have access to these programs. According to the National Institute for Early Education Research—a think tank and research center at Rutgers University—Illinois, Kansas, Michigan, North Carolina, Pennsylvania, Tennessee, Texas, and Virginia open their pre-K programs to children of active duty military families, and to those who have had a parent injured or killed on duty. In Texas, a military child can still attend the program even if there is a change in the parent's duty status.

How Can You Prepare Your Child to Start a New Program?

Some of the same strategies you might use to introduce an older child to a new school also can be used to help your younger child adjust to the new environment.

Ask for a visit or a tour of the program: Before your child spends time in the center or home by herself, ask if you and your child can visit together for an hour or so. Try to pick a time when a few different activities might be taking place, such as circle time, a snack, and free choice, so your child can see the way the teachers organize the day. This will give your child a chance to meet—and maybe play with—some of the other children and adults and might help them adjust more quickly.

Make a photo book: When you visit, take some pictures of your child in the classroom as well as of some of the teachers, toys, books, and play equipment. You can put these in a small album for your child to look at until he or she actually begins attending the center. This might help your child look forward to their first day.

Ask the center to send you some pictures: If you don't get a chance to take your own pictures, ask someone at the center to send you some photos of the classrooms or perhaps of special events they have held for families.

Have your child make a picture for his or her new teacher: Before your child starts at the new center or preschool, ask them to make a picture or a project for their new teacher. Or you can let them pick one of their favorite works that you have been saving. This can give them something to talk about on their first day and avoids some of the complications associated with taking along a favorite toy.

Let the center know if your child has already had more than one child-care provider: If your child has already been in multiple early-childhood settings, let the director or teachers know. A lot of young children—even if they are not in military families—have trouble making the transition to preschool. But information on your child's past experiences—both negative and positive—can help teachers meet your child's learning, social and emotional needs.

Arrange a play date: If possible, arrange a play date with one of the children in the center that you think may become your child's friend. While very young children may sometimes play next to and not with each other, your child may form a connection that will help when they enter the center. Ask the center director if he or she could help with introductions.

Where Can You Find More Information?

Child Care Aware of America, http://www.naccrra.org/military-families: This organization works with the U.S. Military Services to help military families find affordable childcare that suits their unique needs.

Sitter City, https://www.sittercity.com/register_corp_1.html?corp =dod&client=67: Sitter City is a national commercial enterprise that matches parents with babysitters, nannies, child-care programs, and other providers. The Department of Defense is funding membership in this program for military families. It offers profiles that include pictures, parent reviews, references, and background checks. Registration is required.

Military One Source, http://www.militaryonesource.com/default. aspx: This site also has a section on child care issues. Click on Family & Recreation and then Parenting and Child Care.

WHAT IF YOUR CHILD IS IN HIGH SCHOOL?

As mentioned, the challenges associated with changing schools grow more complicated when your children reach high school and are accumulating credits toward graduation. Here are a few issues you might want to consider:

Meet with the counselor: If your new school did not suggest a meeting with the counselor to review the courses your child has already completed, make an appointment as soon as possible. You might find out a required course is missing, and if so, your child will probably need to take that course instead of an elective.

The algebra question: Many states now expect students to complete Algebra 1 in 8th grade, but because your child is changing schools, it's possible that this has been missed. If you are headed to a school where most 9th graders have already had their first year of algebra, but your child has not, make sure this is addressed.

Closely monitor your child's transcript: Stay on top of whether your child is enrolling in the courses he or she needs to be eligible for postsecondary education—not just for a high school diploma. Since you may not know where your child will go to college, it's wise to accumulate additional credits. If only 3 years of math are required, many experts recommend that students take 4 years. Alternatively, if you know where your child wants to go to college, you may want to visit that school's website to familiarize yourself with its requirements. You might also explore whether the state or states in which your child is likely to complete his or her postsecondary education has eligibility criteria that your child must meet to attend a public institution there.

Advanced Placement: With AP courses, students can earn college credit for rigorous courses they complete in high school—a feature that may help them stand out in the college application process and can prevent conflicts over whether courses taken in one state will be accepted in another. The student must pass an AP course exam, usually given toward the end of the school year, in order to earn credit. Colleges, however, vary in what they consider a passing score. Typically a 3 or a 4 is considered passing. Many high schools are now doing a better job of recruiting a diverse pool of students for AP courses, thus creating greater access for students. Ask your school counselor about the AP courses available at your new high school. If the school doesn't have what your child needs, ask about courses available online.

Community college options: Some states will allow students as young as 16 to enroll in courses during the summer at a reduced cost as long as the student's high school approves and there is space in the college course. Some high schools also provide opportunities for dual or joint enrollment. Find out if this is an option for your child. Such academic enrichment opportunities will allow your student to develop or fine-tune his or her skills and knowledge while earning college credit.

Finishing the school year: If your family transfers in the middle of the school year, explore options for allowing your child to complete the school year at his or her current school in order to earn credit for the courses being taken.

School at Home:

Two popular online homeschooling sites are:

- K–12, www.k12.com
- Connections Academy, http://www.connectionsacademy.com/home.aspx

---

Homeschooling or online learning: Some military students are homeschooled–just like many civilian students. Families decide to homeschool their children for a variety of different reasons. For military students, homeschooling can allow them to avoid some of the problems associated with repeating or missing material and wondering whether the courses they have completed will transfer to another state. Online options for accredited homeschooling programs have grown tremendously, allowing students to take their education with them wherever they go. Of course, every child is different, and some thrive as independent learners while others need the routine of going to school every day. Depending on how your child's high school years are unfolding, it might be something to explore. You may also want to explore what types of extracurricular activities are available for homeschooled students in your area.

WHAT OTHER RESOURCES ARE AVAILABLE FOR HIGH SCHOOL MILITARY STUDENTS?

Military Children's Scholarship Handbook: This is published each year by Military Handbooks. It can be downloaded for free. http://www.militaryhandbooks.com/?page_id=106

SAT/ACT PowerPrep: eKnowledge, a group of NFL players, and the Department of Defense have worked together to distribute free SAT/ACT preparation materials to military students. http://eknowledge.com/military.asp

Scholarship Programs of the Fisher House Foundation: The foundation offers a "home away from home" for military families so they can be near a family member who is recovering from an injury. They also have college scholarship programs. http://www.militaryscholar.org/

CHAPTER 2

Policy Matters

This chapter focuses on the role of education policy in supporting military students in public schools. Some of the policies and programs have been put in place to assist other highly mobile students, but could also be adapted for military families. The Common Core education standards and the Common Education Data Standards efforts we describe below would solve some of the problems military families face when they relocate to other states. And in some cases, there are policies and practices designed specifically for military students.

It's important for you to know about these practices, laws, agreements, and proposals. You should be aware of your rights and options in the educational system, or you might take a leadership role in advocating for the full implementation of helpful policies and practices in your state or school district.

This chapter includes information on:

- Meeting the Needs of Military Children with Special Needs
- Common Core State Standards
- Common Education Data Standards
- Lessons from DoDEA Schools
- Impact Aid

MEETING THE NEEDS OF
MILITARY CHILDREN WITH SPECIAL NEEDS

Changing schools frequently can be difficult. If you have a child with a special need, the experience can be even more challenging.

The Individuals with Disabilities Education Act (IDEA) requires that schools provide students with disabilities with a free and appropriate education in the least restrictive environment. Under the IDEA, you work with a team of educators to draft your child's individualized educational program (IEP). An IEP documents your child's disability eligibility status, school- and classroom-based supports, such as testing accommodations, annual academic goals, and other specialized services (e.g., for speech and language) your child might need. An IEP team includes teachers, a school administrator, and other credentialed or designated instructional services staff members, such as an occupational therapist. The IDEA requires that a new IEP be drafted at least annually and a comprehensive evaluation be conducted every 3 years.

In addition, you have the right to call for changes to an existing IEP such as an amendment or to call a meeting to discuss drafting a new plan if you feel the services your child is receiving need to change.

As a military family, you and your child may go through this process multiple times. And as you know, educators in one district may not always see the situation the same way as those in your child's previous school. When meeting with the IEP team, it's also important to communicate to them that because your child is growing up in a military family, he or she may face increased stress or emotional instability that might be contributing to poor learning and behavior outcomes. It is important for educators and other professionals to consider these factors when determining whether a child requires special services.

Timely and Accurate Information

Making sure schools receive as much information as possible in a timely manner is a key to ensuring that your child is served appropriately.

Under IDEA policy, you can call an IEP meeting during the first 30 days your child is in the new school. At this meeting, a new IEP can be drafted to fit the student's needs within the school's existing programs.

But since there are so many issues you have to take care of when you are moving–especially if you or your spouse is deployed–it's possible that this meeting might get overlooked. Contacting the new school before your move can also make the process smoother.

Some school districts such as the Los Angeles Unified School District utilize a secured online system to track current and past IEPs. These tracking systems assist schools in identifying incoming students with IEPs and monitoring the progress of current students with IEPs. However, not all school districts have an online tracking system, and often, incoming students with IEPs are not identified in advance, so you need to make sure your child's needs are being addressed.

There are other practical steps you can take to make sure there is a smooth transition between schools. You can assist the school's identification process by:

- keeping copies of all your child's records
- submitting a copy of the IEP to the special education teacher and administrator
- meeting with the school's special education teacher or coordinator to discuss the IEP's implementation
- keeping copies of the district's special education policies and procedures manual.

The Exceptional Family Member Program

As a military parent of a child with a special need, you are required to enroll in your branch's Exceptional Family Member Program (EFMP). As part of the program, the special needs of your child are considered in determining Permanent Change of Station assignments. EFMP works with other military and civilian agencies to provide community support, housing, educational, medical, and personnel services to families with special needs. This program, however, is independent from school special education programs and there may be limited communication between the two–especially in school districts not located near a military installation.

Some installations have an EFMP liaison who can assist you in both enrolling in the program and working with your school to make sure your child receives the services he or she needs.

In addition, parent advocacy groups and other resources are available to help you understand and navigate the system.

Other resources:

- **STOMP**, which stands for Specialized Training of Military Parents, is a nationwide parent training and information center. The project aims to "empower military parents, individuals with disabilities, and service providers with knowledge, skills, and resources so that they might access services to create a collaborative environment for family and professional partnerships without regard to geographic location." One component of President Obama's "Strengthening Our Military Families" directive is to continue the implementation of the STOMP initiative. http://www.stompproject.org/
- The **MilitaryHOMEFRONT** website provides a listing of EFMP/special needs contacts for all military installations both in the United States and overseas. http://www. militaryhomefront.dod.mil/portal/page/mhf/MHF/MHF_ DETAIL_1?section_id=20.40.500.570.0.0.0.0.0&content_ id=180334
- **Military OneSource.com** offers a special section of its website on understanding the early intervention and special education process in public schools. Click on the "Career and Education" tab. http://www.militaryonesource.mil
- **Planning Your Child's Transition to Preschool: A Step-by-Step Guide for Families** is a publication from the University of Illinois at Urbana-Champaign. It focuses on preparing for the transition from early intervention services for children with disabilities to preschool or other educational services at age 3. While it is not written specifically for military families, it offers some examples of family situations and covers issues that parents with young children need to be considering if they are preparing for a move. http://facts.crc.uiuc.edu/facts4/facts4.html

COMMON CORE STATE STANDARDS

When military children attend one of the 194 DoDEA schools around the world—whether it's McBride Elementary on Ft. Benning in Georgia or Boeblingen Elementary in Heidelberg, Germany—they are taught the same curriculum, and are assessed using the same tests, which allows for comparisons among students.

This uniformity is in place so that military children, who often must pick up and change schools with little advance preparation, won't fall behind in school, or even have to repeat material that they've already covered. This creates a predictable situation for families who may have unpredictable lives.

The same is not true in civilian schools. Currently in the United States, each state sets its own standards for what students are expected to learn as they progress through school. But this system has led to wide variation across the country, and students—not just those in the military, but anyone who moves from state to state—sometimes experience redundancy in lessons or far worse, miss out on entire subjects.

The Common Core State Standards is an effort led by two national organizations—the Council of Chief State School Officers and the National Governors Association—to develop clear and consistent guidelines for what students are expected to learn and to prepare them for college and careers.

The Common Core, in effect, mirrors the approach already used by the DoDEA schools. Supporters of the Common Core, which the Obama administration is urging states to adopt, say that in addition to allowing for comparison of student performance across the country, the Core also makes it easier for educators to share best practices about instruction.

Accommodating the needs of military students—and other highly mobile populations—was actually part of the rationale behind the development of the Common Core.

In a letter of endorsement, Mary M. Keller, the president and CEO of the Military Child Education Coalition, wrote about why the initiative makes sense for military students.

"As military assignments or family circumstances resulting from a parent's deployment lead to school moves, parents and students need to be confident that these transitions will not increase turbulence in students' lives or endanger their opportunity to achieve," she wrote. "They also need to know that no matter where they attend school, they will have the chance to master those concepts and skills that ensure successful study at the post-secondary level and prepare them to enter the world of work."

If all states adopt the Common Core State Standards, this would address many of the obstacles that military children moving between installations in the United States currently face, such as repeating or missing academic material and transferring credit for courses taken.

At the time of publication, 45 states had adopted the Common Core.

While not yet implemented across all states, the Common Core State Standards provide some solutions for military students—and others that relocate often—that can minimize the disruption in their educational progress.

COMMON EDUCATION DATA STANDARDS

Military families are keenly aware that states and even local school districts vary tremendously in regards to the information they require when a new student enrolls in school. But clearly military families are not the only ones who move from state to state and have to cope with record-keeping procedures that were different in their previous school.

That's why the Common Education Data Standards (CEDS) initiative was launched—to create data on preschool, K–12 and K–12 to postsecondary that could be easily compared and understood from state to state. One presentation by the initiative describes it as creating "an integrated profile of each learner that can be passed seamlessly" among institutions and between states.

Partners in the effort include the National Center for Education Statistics, several state and local education agencies, the Council of

Chief State School Officers, State Higher Education Executive Officers, and other organizations that focus on education data.

One recent example that emphasized the need for common data standards is Hurricane Katrina, after which thousands of students were forced to disperse to other states and districts across the southern United States, creating a pressing need for administrators and teachers in their new schools to quickly and accurately obtain their records and place them in classes appropriately.

This scenario is nothing new for military parents and students. The CEDS effort is voluntary and is still a work in progress. While it wasn't solely designed with military families in mind, the CEDS responds to many of the complications military children face when changing schools on short notice.

To learn more about the initiative, visit: http://www.commoned datastandards.org/

LESSONS FROM DoDEA SCHOOLS

If your children have ever attended one of 194 schools operated by the Department of Defense Education Activity (DoDEA), you know that these schools were created to specifically respond to the needs of highly mobile military children. But that doesn't mean civilian school districts with military students can't learn from some of their practices.

In their 2003 study, "It's a Way of Life for Us: High Mobility and High Achievement in Department of Defense Schools," Vanderbilt University researchers Claire E. Smrekar and Debra E. Owens suggest that DoDEA has created a culture of high expectations for students that is complemented by treating high mobility as "a way of life" rather than a problem that can't be solved.

Student Records

For schools with high student turnover, the timely transfer of student records is one of the greatest challenges. DoDEA schools have created a standardized process to ensure that there is as little delay as possible in students' learning.

"We put a lot of focus on trying to get a lot of information to the next school before the student arrives," says Mike Lynch, the chief of policy and legislation at DoDEA.

At the elementary level, parents carry their child's official records by hand to the next school, while the sending school keeps a copy.

At the middle and high school level, a student's transcript is electronically transferred to the receiving school—allowing for no interruption in educational services.

DoDEA schools have also worked to eliminate what Lynch calls "homegrown" forms—those locally created documents or permission slips that you are often required to complete in order for your child to be enrolled.

Lynch adds that when a student is transferring to another DoDEA school, teachers or school administrators often communicate with the receiving school if they think there is a particular educational or adjustment issue that could create problems for the child at the new school.

Communication between DoDEA and civilian schools, when a child is transferring from one to the other, is not that common, however. Lynch described this communication as "episodic, random, and rare." If the school your child is moving to hasn't offered to contact the previous school, you can make that suggestion, particularly if there are any issues that you think need to be addressed.

Finally, the fact that all DoDEA schools use the same curriculum helps to ensure that students won't fall behind during a move—even if they are in one DoDEA school in Germany on a Friday and enter another one in North Carolina the following Monday.

Student Support

DoDEA schools also build their school climate around the fact that students—and parents—are always on the move.

When a student comes in to a DoDEA school to register, the schools actually prefer that the student wait a day or two before coming to school, explains Patricia A. Cassiday, the former coordinator for counseling and psychological services for DoDEA.

That gives the teacher time to get a desk, books and other materials ready for the student. It also gives the class a chance to prepare to welcome the new student. The scene is more of a "celebration instead of 'oh no, another student,'" Cassiday says.

An appointment with the school counselor is usually scheduled as soon as the student is enrolled. Again, if the school your child is entering doesn't currently have such a practice in place, you can always request a meeting.

In the classroom, teachers are trained to differentiate instruction to meet students' individual learning needs. Even though all DoDEA schools use the same curriculum, many students have still been in a variety of classrooms and have encountered different experiences that could affect whether they are meeting the standards for their grade.

If a large deployment takes place, the school community will often hold a barbecue or some other event for the families. This is not only a way to recognize the servicemen and women, but also allows the schools to see how the spouses remaining behind are handling the transition. They might say they don't need support, Cassiday says, but they will attend something that is organized for their children.

Then, when a child is preparing to move on, the class or school offers some gesture to make the student feel appreciated. It can be as simple as a certificate, a T-shirt, or a pillowcase signed by all of the student's classmates. It's a way to say, "thank you for being part of our school community," Cassiday says. This is a gesture any school can make.

IMPACT AID

Impact Aid, created in 1950, is a program funded by the federal government and intended to pay back school districts when they lose a portion of their tax revenue base because federal property—such as a military installation—is located within their boundaries. In some cases, school districts are entirely located on a military base. In addition to

This unique lifestyle imposed on military children highlights the need to ensure that schools serving our children have the finest teachers, facilities and support structure that our nation can afford. Impact Aid was meant to do this.

—*Impact Aid: Providing for the Educational Needs of Military Families,* Military Impacted Schools Association

losing property taxes, these districts might also lose sales taxes and other fees because military families can shop at stores (commissaries or exchanges) that don't charge taxes.

Impact Aid funds go directly to school districts, which have freedom in how they use the money—purchasing textbooks or other resources, for computers, utilities, and even hiring teachers. The funds are not specifically allocated to be used for military students, although a school could decide to use them this way. The program, however, is not "forward funded," meaning that from year to year, school districts don't know how much Congress will appropriate for the program.

Over time, the program has been expanded to include other "federally connected" children, such as those living in subsidized housing, on tribal lands, or in national parks. That means less of the funding is used for military students.

Eligibility and Funding

In order to receive Impact Aid, at least 400 students or 3% of a school's enrollment must be federally connected. Schools receive more money from the program if their military students live on a base than if they live in the community.

Schools determine how many military students—or other federally connected students—they have by conducting a survey or by doing a parent's employment "source check." These results are then used to fill out an Impact Aid application.

Some school administrators don't apply for these funds, however, because they don't want to question parents about whether they are in the military. *Not doing so, however, means your school is losing federal money.*

As a military parent, it is important for you to fill out these surveys so your school can get an accurate count and receive these additional funds. Likewise, if your school is not receiving Impact Aid–and you know there are a lot of military children in your school–urge your school administrators to conduct these surveys and apply for these funds.

In addition to basic payments, the program provides funds for construction-related expenses, including debt repayments on school additions or new buildings. A grant program is also available to schools where at least 40% of the students are from military families or federally connected.

Up until 1970, the Impact Aid program was fully funded. But in the middle of that year, the funding was cut in half and has never been completely restored. The program is currently funded at 60% of the need.

Reform Proposals

Recent recommendations focusing on Impact Aid reauthorization have focused on making sure federally impacted districts receive their payments in a "more timely fashion," increasing efficiency in the program and ensuring that districts don't receive less than in previous years. Early childhood education advocates have also recommended that Impact Aid funds be used for preschool programs.

Resources

The following organizations provide more detailed information on the Impact Aid program:

- The U.S. Department of Education provides official information on Impact Aid. http://www2.ed.gov/about/offices/list/oese/impactaid/index.html

2. Policy Matters

- The Military Impacted Schools Association has a series of resources available on its website, including a video, a PowerPoint presentation, and a booklet. Click on MISA. http://militaryimpactedschoolsassociation.org/
- The National Association of Federally Impacted Schools also provides information. Click on the "Basics" tab. http://www.nafisdc.org/

CHAPTER 3

Deployment

If you or your spouse has deployed or is about to be deployed, you know that the routine you have created for your children at home is about to turn upside down. In addition to thinking about household and financial responsibilities that will need to be taken care of during this time, consider the ways that this deployment will affect your children's performance in school.

Military families are often encouraged to make a pre-deployment checklist. You should also make a *school checklist* for this deployment period. This list may include important points that schools should know about in order to support your child during this time.

Checklist questions might include:

- If you are the parent who typically helps with homework, how will that now be handled?
- How is my child responding to the news of this deployment?
- If my spouse is deployed, am I also working during this time?
- Who will get the child to and from school? Does the child ride the bus or does he or she need to start riding the bus?
- Will my child need before- and after-school care? Is homework help available?
- If you are deployed, how involved do you think you can be in your child's education? Do you want to be included in parent-teacher meetings by phone or teleconference, or do you want the parent at home to handle those meetings?
- If your child misses a day of school to say goodbye or to see a parent home on leave, how will the school treat this absence? Can the school provide class work in advance? Can work that is missed be made up?

Decision Point:
To Inform or Not to Inform

Should you tell the school that someone in your family is being deployed? It's possible that your family has weathered deployments in the past without any negative effects on your child, but every deployment is different and you can't always predict how your child will respond to the most recent deployment. Informing your child's teachers or a counselor that a parent has been sent on a mission—possibly for as long as 18 months—will help them monitor how your child is doing in the classroom and plan ways to be supportive.

- If both parents are deploying, is the child's caregiver fully informed about school schedules, homework procedures, and other expectations? Has the school been informed who will be responsible for the child during this time? How much authority will this person have to make decisions regarding schoolwork?

HOW CAN YOU SUPPORT YOUR CHILD ACADEMICALLY DURING THIS DEPLOYMENT?

If you are the parent still at home, how much are you expecting the child to help with household duties? All members of a family should contribute to keeping the home running smoothly, but a child's primary "job" is to be a student. If added responsibilities, such as chores and taking care of younger siblings, are cutting into the time your child needs for homework and studying, he or she could fall behind in class. Likewise, if there is no longer time for leisure activities, spending time with friends, or extracurricular activities, your child is missing out on experiences that can help him or her weather this time without one of his or her parents.

Is your child missing more days of school than usual? In times of stress, parents are often advised to maintain routine for children. And that includes regular attendance at school. Understand that children might be missing school because they want to avoid questions about their deployed parent. Other children may feel that they need to stay home to help you and take care of you if you are having a hard time or seem sad.

What about block leave? If the service member in your family will be on leave during the school year, discuss this in advance with your child's teacher(s) to determine how many days of school your child can reasonably miss in order to spend time with the parent who is coming home. If the school doesn't have a written policy regarding block leave, find out how those absences will be treated—as excused or unexcused. Ask for a packet of class work to be sent home in advance or see if assignments can be submitted by e-mail. Some school districts only allow a certain number of absences during the year, so make sure you are clear on these rules in advance.

Is your child allowed to work ahead on assignments? Some teachers assign a packet of homework at the beginning of the week, allowing students to complete this at their own pace. Getting it done early in the week can make the rest of the afternoons and evenings run smoother, especially if you have children in more than one grade or if they have afternoon activities. If your children's teachers don't do this, see if they might start, or see how many assignments they can let you know about in advance.

Does your child seem distracted or disengaged in school? When one parent is gone, home life often feels disorganized. That disorganization can also affect a child's schoolwork. Does your child seem distracted? Is he or she missing assignments or forgetting homework? Organization skills come naturally for some children, while others have to work hard at it—especially in making the transition from elementary to middle school. Make special efforts to have a place at

3. Deployment

home for your child to do homework and to keep their books and other school supplies. If your school doesn't provide students with a calendar or an organizer, purchase or make one yourself.

Are your child's grades declining? If you see a noticeable difference in how your child is performing in school, ask for a meeting with a teacher or counselor, or send an email to express your concern. You should not have to wait until a scheduled parent-teacher conference. If the teacher is also noticing a pattern, ask for suggestions and explore what services the school might have for tutoring or additional help for your child.

Are your child's teachers communicating with you or are they worried about bothering you? Did your child get in trouble at school, or get sent to the nurse's office, but you didn't get a phone call? It's possible that the staff at your child's school is trying so hard not to create more stress for your family during a deployment that they aren't involving you in everything that is happening with your child. Try to stay in close contact with someone at the school so they feel comfortable keeping you informed. Note that some teachers and administrators tend to contact parents only when a child is in trouble. Help them understand how important it is for you and for your child to hear about your child's strengths and accomplishments.

Should you move to be closer to friends and family? Many military families move during a lengthy deployment to be near family members or friends who can assist in caring for the children and serve as a support system. But consider how such a move will impact your children's education. Have they already changed schools repeatedly? How are they doing in their current school? Are they in a school that has a lot of other military children who understand what it's like to be a military child? Is it possible that you can find the support you need without moving?

Can you work with other military families to help students with deployed parents? If a deployment is affecting a large number of students in your school at the same time, consider working with school leaders to accommodate the needs of these students. Schools may change certain routines, plan in advance, and be more flexible when they realize that a large group of families and parents are being affected. They might look for special grants to create tutoring programs or recruit long-term volunteers so that the needs of these students and families are met. Again, maybe you have the support you need from family members or friends, but by working as a group, you could provide solutions for families that might be struggling.

WHAT SUPPORT DOES YOUR CHILD NEED SOCIALLY AND EMOTIONALLY?

Are support networks and services available? Military families who use the support services and networks available to them are better equipped to handle the schoolwork, activities, household duties, and other demands during a deployment. Look for opportunities to carpool to after-school activities, seek out homework help programs, and take advantage of deployment support groups. Even if you are feeling in control of everything, you might be a helpful friend to another military spouse. If you are a National Guard or Reservist family, you may not have access to the same family support services available to active duty military families, so it might be even more necessary to communicate with your child's teacher(s) about the deployment and let them offer suggestions for lightening the burden.

Is your child involved in any fun activities either at school or in the community? If your child begins to pull away from the activities he or she enjoys, or doesn't have time for fun because of added responsibilities at home, this could lead to resentment or social-emotional problems later.

Is your child eating well? Proper nutrition can contribute to improved performance in school and affect a child's mood. You may want to consider preparing meals ahead of time to keep school nights from getting stressful because of homework and other responsibilities. Cooking meals together is an activity enjoyed in many families, and children tend to eat better when they are the ones helping to make the meal.

Does your child have an outlet for expression? Just as you might feel overwhelmed at times when the family is separated, your children can feel the effects of a deployment, but may not know how to express their feelings. Art, music, dance, and other visual and performing arts are vehicles for expressing emotions that might be uncomfortable to discuss. Even if these programs exist in the schools your children attend, they might also need additional opportunities after school or during the summer to delve further into these activities without worrying about earning a certain grade. Consult local parks and recreation departments, which may offer classes that are more affordable than private programs.

Some national military organizations allow students to express themselves through blogs and forums. For instance, Operation Military Kids (http://www.operationmilitarykids.org/public/stories.aspx) invites children to share their stories. Children who enjoy writing might appreciate this opportunity. Here's one example: Tori (12) from Colorado says, "Many people outside of military families do not understand how hard it is to have a parent away. My dad and mom both served in the Navy. My mom was discharged after serving seven years and now raises us kids. Growing up I remember moving around from Navy base to Navy base. I spent three years in California then another four years in Hawaii. Like most kids, my dad was deployed a lot."

WHERE CAN YOU FIND ADDITIONAL INFORMATION?

Deployment Tips: This site from the Military Health System lists contacts for programs to support families from all branches during deployments. http://fhp.osd.mil/deploymentTips.jsp#service

Surviving Deployment.com: This site provides ideas for activities, links to other resources, and helpful articles, such as "Helping Children Handle Deployments." http://www.survivingdeployment.com/articles.html

SOFAR: Strategic Outreach to Families of All Reservists aids families of Army Reservists and members of the National Guard. SOFAR is a mental health project that provides free psychological support, psychotherapy, psychoeducation, and prevention services to extended family members before and after a deployment. http://www.sofarusa.org/index.html

Military Deployment Guide: Preparing You and Your Family for the Road Ahead: This handbook includes a series of questions focusing on how the deployment might affect children. http://cs.mhf.dod.mil/content/dav/mhf/QOL-Library/Project%20Documents/MilitaryHOMEFRONT/Service%20Providers/Deployment/2011_DeploymentGuide.pdf

Deployment: This page on the National Military Family Association website is divided into four sections: Managing and Preparing, Reunion, Back at Home, and Support Groups. http://www.militaryfamily.org/get-info/deployment/

The Yellow Ribbon Program: Specifically for members of the National Guard and Reserves, this program provides information on benefits and referrals before, during, and after deployments. Its Center for Excellence provides "lessons learned" on a variety of issues, including a "Children's Curriculum" area that includes activities for children during deployment periods and reunions. http://www.yellowribbon.mil/

Operation Healthy Reunions: An effort of Mental Health America, this provides education and resources aimed at eliminating the stigma of mental health issues among soldiers and their families. Topics covered include reuniting with your spouse and children, adjusting after war, and PTSD. http://www.nmha.org/reunions/resources.cfm#4

3. Deployment

Helping Children Cope with Deployments and Reunions: This is a section on the Real Warriors website that discusses preparing children for and supporting them through each phase of deployment. Real Warriors is a campaign designed to promote resilience and recovery among returning service members, veterans, and their families. http://www.realwarriors.net/family/children/deployment.php

How to Prepare Your Children and Stay Involved in Their Education During Deployment: This booklet from the Military Child Education Coalition offers suggestions for both parents and educators and provides insight into some of the thoughts and feelings that children might have surrounding a parent's deployment. The free download is available in MCEC's online library. http://www.militarychild.org/library

Helping Children Cope with the Challenges of War and Terrorism: This workbook provides activities for adults and children to identify, understand, and cope with their feelings. http://www.7-dippity.com/other/UWA_war_book.pdf

ARE THERE SUPPORT RESOURCES
GEARED TOWARD CHILDREN?

Talk, Listen, Connect: This is an initiative of Sesame Workshop, the organization behind *Sesame Street*. In partnership with Walmart and The New York Office of Mental Health, the effort helps young children of military members cope with feelings, challenges, and concerns related to deployment. The site offers videos featuring popular Muppet characters as well as other materials. http://www.sesameworkshop.org/what-we-do/our-work/reaching-out-to-military-families-6-detail.html

More Changes? Are You Kidding Me?: As part of its Coming Together Around Military Families initiative, the Zero to Three organization provides this short, two-page flier about reunification for

parents of infants and toddlers. http://www.zerotothree.org/about-us/
funded-projects/military-families/flyer3.pdf.

Deployment Kids: This site offers games, puzzles, and activities
for military children. http://www.deploymentkids.com/playtime.html

United Through Reading: This service offers DVDs of deployed
parents reading books aloud to their children. There is also a book,
You're Never Far Away, that can be customized with the service member's branch of the military and the child's name. http://www.
unitedthroughreading.org/military/

Military Deployment and Families: This audio is part of the Healthy
Children initiative of the American Academy of Pediatrics. http://
www.healthychildren.org/English/family-life/family-dynamics/
pages/Military-Deployment-and-Families.aspx

A Backpack Journalist: Based in Houston, this company plans
workshops and events for children and teens to help them through
the deployment cycle. Using different media in a mobile lab, children
learn to express themselves and connect with their family members
and other youth. The company also offers an internship program in
which military youth complete a course and then assist teachers in the
program. http://www.abackpackjournalist.com/

My Life: A Kid's Journal: This is the second of three journals
from TRICARE for children. It is designed to help children with a deployed parent express their emotions throughout the various stages of
the experience. https://www.hnfs.net/content/hnfs/home/tn/bene/
res/symbolic_links/kids_journals.html

Tell Me a Story: The Military Child Education Coalition developed this program to empower military children "by using literature
and their own stories in a way that fosters skills for resilience, strong
peer and parent connections, a sense of pride and accomplishment,
and a caring community." Families gather for a Tell Me a Story event

at their school, in which they hear the featured book and then break into small groups for discussion and activities with a group leader. At the end of the evening, families receive their own copy of the book. If your school hasn't tried this program, you might want to suggest it to a teacher or administrator. http://www.militarychild.org/parents-and-students/programs/tell-me-a-story-tmas.

CHAPTER 4

Traumatic Experiences

Being in a military family can expose your children to stressful situations or upsetting topics that civilian children may never encounter.

Many children are naturally resilient and will learn how to cope with each transition and change in their lives. But others may face social and emotional troubles and will need more individualized attention and care.

If you have more than one child, you know how different children can be from one another. Just because one child adjusted easily following a recent move and quickly made friends at his or her new school doesn't mean his or her siblings will sail through with the same ease.

In addition, as mentioned earlier, each family move and each deployment happens at a different stage in a child's life. Just because your child handled previous changes well doesn't mean he or she will always have the strength and skills to bounce right back.

Some particular families may experience events that are much more stressful and traumatic than those commonly shared by all military families. Injury, loss, and a parent's post-traumatic stress are a few of the more extreme experiences faced by some military children.

As a parent, you can best support your children by anticipating the transitions that they will be experiencing, recognizing that each transition holds the potential for disruptions, and being keenly aware of how traumatic events in your family impact your child. Make yourself aware of support services both through the military, in the community, and at your children's schools.

As mentioned in earlier chapters, your child's school—or at least his or her teachers—should play a role in supporting your child through difficult times. They want your child to succeed in the classroom, so informing them of the changes at home that could affect performance in school benefits both your child and the teacher.

This does not mean that your child needs to be singled out for counseling, special education, or a support group that may or may not provide comfort. But it can mean that teachers or other professionals at the school are made aware of the situations or topics that are upsetting your child and have strategies in place to provide support and comfort.

If the school is not offering assistance or doesn't have counselors or school social workers who can meet with you or your child—or at least monitor how the child is adjusting—you will need to take more of an advocacy role and educate your school on how to assist military students experiencing difficult times or trauma at home.

Here are some questions that you might be having:

What if the school is not responsive to your concerns? Place a call to the district office. Ask to speak with a school psychologist or social worker. Districts across the country have faced significant budget reductions, and unfortunately counselors, school nurses, and other support positions at the school level are often the first positions to be cut. If your school doesn't have a counselor, ask to be referred to someone at the district level.

What if your child is experiencing extreme stress and anxiety related to moving and leaving friends or traumatic events? New friends can't replace old friends, especially as children get older and their peer group becomes increasingly important. As mentioned earlier, Facebook, with the appropriate security settings in place, can allow them to stay connected on even a daily basis to the friends they have met across the country and around the world. In time, most children will also begin to make friends at their new schools. For younger children, sports, after-school classes, and other outside school activities can also speed the process of helping children form new relationships. In addition, check in with the teacher often to see whether your child is forming friendships at school. Your children might still tell you that they are miserable about leaving their previous home, but in reality, they might be adjusting well. If your child is not building new relationships, ask if the school provides any support groups or transition activities for new students or for military students.

What if your child doesn't want to go to school? Allowing your child to skip a day or more because he or she is struggling emotionally sets up a bad pattern that your child will try to take advantage of over and over again. Your child may try to avoid school by saying they feel sick, or they may truly be experiencing physical symptoms because of the anxiety they are facing about attending the new school. Involve your pediatrician to rule out any possible illnesses.

Also, let your children know that they might not only face consequences from you if they don't get out of bed, but that unexcused absences could also result in a detention at school or loss of eligibility to participate in sports or clubs.

Let them know that staying home and missing class work will only make it harder for them to keep up. More importantly, be up front with the school about this issue. A teacher may be able to provide insight into what is happening at school that your child wants to avoid. Even request a home visit from a teacher, counselor, or administrator if the school hasn't taken this step. That personal contact might be necessary to jolt the child into recognizing the seriousness of the issue.

- This article from EmpoweringParents.com provides suggestions on ways to provide incentives for regular attendance. http://www.empoweringparents.com/i-don't-want-to-go-to-school.php#
- This Kidshealth.org website speaks to children about their feelings regarding not wanting to go to school. http://kidshealth.org/kid/feeling/school/hate_school.html

4. Traumatic Experiences

What if your child is experiencing extreme stress or anxiety related to a family member's deployment or injury? Again, keeping teachers or others at the school informed about significant events, such as a mother's or father's deployment, can only assist them in being prepared to provide support or seek expertise from district-level or community-based mental health professionals. Let them know if the unit the child's parent serves in has experienced loss of life or serious injuries. Make sure they know when the unit is returning so they can prepare for any reactions from your child.

Then if your child becomes distracted in school or is easily upset, they will know why. Your child might have trouble focusing because they are constantly thinking about a loved one being in a far-away place where the unknown challenges and obstacles of war are occurring. This can keep them from concentrating on schoolwork—especially if they have been out of contact with the deployed parent or relative.

Consult frequently with teachers about whether lessons or homework should be adapted to allow assignments to be completed in smaller chunks. Children need to learn ways to take control of their fears and recognize they can still accomplish their work and participate in activities in spite of being concerned for someone's safety.

Some schools have developed programs to increase children's resilience and coping skills. The FOCUS program, described below, is a great example. Check whether your school has such a group, and if so, ask how your child can be included. If not, this is another area in which military parents can advocate for services for their children. The website for our project (http://buildingcapacity.usc.edu/) is another resource for finding programs and practices that your school could implement.

Attend a school event, such as a play, a game, or a curriculum night, to give you and your child a pleasant experience at the school. This can help the school seem more friendly and supportive. It might also provide a good opportunity for casual conversation with your child's teachers.

What if a parent has been seriously injured? As soon as possible, let the school know the circumstances and whether any rehabilitation the military member is receiving requires your family to relocate, even temporarily. In this case, the child might not be missing school because they want to, but because events outside your control require it. Ask about independent study arrangements if the child will miss a lot of school.

Accommodating Parents with Disabilities

In addition to having ramps for wheelchairs, as required by law, here are a few other things schools can do to include parents with disabilities:

- If a parent's vision has been affected, ask that school materials be provided in large print, on a CD, or in Braille.
- If a parent can no longer write, ask that they be allowed to give verbal consent for official documents instead of a signature.
- If the parent has lost hearing, ask that the school communicate in writing instead of by phone. Ask for scripts of school plays or written lyrics of songs being performed.
- Let the school know if a service dog is accompanying a disabled parent.
- If the parent has mobility issues, is an elevator available if the school has more than one floor?

Source: NI Direct-Official government website for Northern Ireland. http://www.nidirect.gov.uk/index/information-and-services/people-with-disabilities/disabled-parents/disabled-parents-and-school.htm

On a more long-term basis, if the parent becomes permanently disabled, recognize that your child's relationship with the injured parent will be affected. They might not be able to play together in the same way or do the same activities, including school projects or homework. This might make your child confused or angry depending on his or her age. Look for ways that your child can still positively interact with both parents, emphasizing the parents' abilities instead of disabilities and the mutual support and love of the family.

What if the reintegration phase is not going well? If you or a family member is experiencing significant stress, anger, depression, thoughts of violence or suicide, or other psychological trauma related to re-entry, those feelings can also have an effect on the children in the home.

4. Traumatic Experiences

Children may become afraid to say anything that they think might trigger a negative outburst, including discussing issues related to schoolwork. They might have trouble sleeping or have bad dreams because of stress in the home, which could affect how well they are functioning in school. And they might withdraw from extracurricular activities out of concern for you or because they don't want to face questions or comments about their family from peers or other adults. A child can even begin to experience the same symptoms as the parent who actually experienced the war-related trauma firsthand. In order to protect their family, children also may avoid sharing information with school staff about troubles at home. They also might

---

Families OverComing Under Stress (FOCUS)

Based at the University of California, Los Angeles, FOCUS is a resiliency training program for military children and families. Participants learn how to handle the challenges of deployment and reintegration. The program teaches:

- emotional regulation
- communication
- problem solving
- goal setting
- managing deployment reminders

There is also a version of FOCUS for families with young children, in response to research showing that even infants and toddlers can experience stress and depression. FOCUS for Early Childhood emphasizes the parent-child relationship. Family sessions are used to model and practice skills. The three main components of FOCUS for Early Childhood are psychoeducation, creating a family narrative/timeline, and skills training in the areas of emotional regulation, communication, problem solving, and goal setting.

The FOCUS program is available at many installations across the country and in Japan. In addition, online training is available. More information can be found at http://www.focusproject.org/.

be afraid to complain about something a military parent has done because others in the community recognize him or her only as a hero.

Seek professional help through the military health care service, faith-based counselors, or other community organizations. Maintain communication with children's teachers to find out whether the child is missing assignments, withdrawing from friends, or displaying behavior problems. Ask about tutoring opportunities if the child is falling behind, or school clubs that could provide additional support and stress relief.

What if the school wants your child to receive special education services? If teachers don't know that a child is reacting to stressful situations at home, poor performance in school or emotional or behavioral problems may only indicate to them that the child needs to be tested for special education services. This is why it is important to keep the school informed about the experiences he or she has had as a military child, especially if your child is new to the school or if there are gaps in your child's records from previous schools.

Dealing with any trauma that your child is going through should be carefully considered as part of any discussions with educators about testing your child.

Short-term accommodations in the general classroom can be made for children under Section 504 of the Rehabilitation Act. This might be an option to discuss with school officials. A section of the U.S. Department of Education website explains the differences between special education and a 504 plan. http://www2.ed.gov/about/offices/list/ocr/504faq.html

What if your family has experienced a loss? The death of a spouse is a horrible event that changes your family forever. This book is not intended to provide all of the support and healing you will need if you have suffered such a tragedy. Our intention is to focus on just one aspect of life after loss—interaction with your child's school.

A death affects not only your family, but the school your child attends as well. If the school wants to honor the child's parent in some way—such as by holding a memorial service, hanging a plaque,

4. Traumatic Experiences

or planting a tree—allowing them to show their respect can help the child feel comforted and valued during such a traumatic time. But if your child doesn't want that kind of attention right away, talk with the school about postponing their displays until your child feels ready.

If your child has been out of school for awhile following the death, ask to meet with teachers or a counselor before he or she returns to school to discuss what the child might need and to help ease the transition back into a school routine. Depending on your child's age, he or she can be involved in the meeting.

On a more long-term basis, it's important to stay in contact with your child's teachers or another professional at the school regarding how your child is functioning in class and whether accommodations need to be made in schoolwork, whether behavior is changing, how teachers are handling the child's grief, and if ongoing counseling is necessary. A teacher, coach, counselor, or other staff member who listens and cares for your child following such a tragedy can be part of your support system as well.

If you as the surviving parent are not able to make these requests of the school or attend these meetings, consult with a school liaison officer, a relative, or a close friend who can serve as an intermediary.

WHAT OTHER RESOURCES ARE AVAILABLE?

Parents Trauma Resource Center: This site from the National Institute for Trauma and Loss in Children provides detailed information about grief and trauma, including the difference between grief and trauma, ways that parents can help their children and themselves, specific information for different age groups, and ways to handle specific issues such as behavioral problems, sexual abuse, war, and terrorism. The site also offers specific activities to help children understand and work through their grief or trauma. http://tlcinstitute.org/PTRC.html

"Children of Wounded Warriors: Guidance for Caregivers": This article from eXtension—which presents research and knowledge from land-grant universities across the United States—suggests

ways to help children prepare for and adjust to a parent's serious injury. http://www.extension.org/pages/60148/children-of-wounded -warriors:-guidance-for-caregivers

Helping Children Cope with Loss, Death, and Grief: Tips for Teachers and Parents: This article from the National Association of School Psychologists provides advice to parents on how to handle the issues of death and grief in the classroom. http://nasponline.org/ resources/crisis_safety/griefwar.pdf

2010 Revised Handbook for Injured Service Members and Their Families: This resource is published by the Intrepid Fallen Heroes Fund. The purpose is to assist injured service members and their families by providing information about what to expect, an overview of resources at their disposal, and a discussion of certain issues they are likely to confront. It is designed to supplement the information provided directly by the various branches of the military, as well as by governmental and nongovernmental organizations. http://fallenheroesfund.org/Family-Resources.aspx

Tragedy Assistance Program for Survivors: This organization provides around-the-clock services for military families, such as emotional support, crisis intervention, grief and trauma resources, and "Good Grief" camps for children. http://www.taps.org/

Resources for Wounded or Injured Service Members and Their Families: This fact sheet from the National Military Family Association provides basic definitions and information on procedures related to wounded warriors. http://support.militaryfamily.org/site/ DocServer/Wounded_Servicemember7-06.pdf?docID=6703

The National Institute for Trauma and Loss in Children: This organization provides direct services to traumatized children and families as well as resource materials. The website features a series of podcasts featuring professionals who have worked with military families regarding deployment and other experiences. http://www. starrtraining.org/tlc

4. Traumatic Experiences

Parent Guide: Supporting a Grieving Child: This handbook comes from the National Center for School Crisis and Bereavement. It includes suggestions on how children respond to death, helping children understand, cope over time, and taking care of yourself. http://www.cincinnatichildrens.org/svc/alpha/s/school-crisis/parent-guide.htm

Returning from the War Zone: The Department of Veterans Affairs has released an interactive guide for families that includes video clips of families dealing with the challenges of reintegration following deployment to war. A PDF version including family stories is also available. http://www.ptsd.va.gov/public/reintegration/returning_from_the_war_zone_guides.asp

ARE THERE TRAUMA OR GRIEF RESOURCES SPECIFICALLY FOR CHILDREN?

Talk, Listen, Connect: This is an initiative of Sesame Workshop, the organization behind *Sesame Street.* In partnership with Walmart and The New York Office of Mental Health, the effort includes videos and other materials focused on helping young children of military members cope with grief. http://www.sesameworkshop.org/what-we-do/our-work/reaching-out-to-military-families-6-detail.html

My Life Continued is a bereavement journal for military children who have lost a parent or loved one who served in the military. The journal is a private place to write down thoughts and feelings and was created to help children remember and honor their loved one and help them apply that love in a productive way as they move forward in their lives. https://www.hnfs.net/content/dam/hnfs/tn/common/pdf/Bereav_Journal.pdf

The Dougy Center: This site offers activities for grieving children such as open-ended sentences and drawing suggestions. http://www.dougy.org/grief-resources/activities/

THE HEROES' TREE

The Heroes' Tree is one practice that a school can use to honor both living and deceased members of the military. The community initiative recognizes and honors both current and past members of the Armed Forces. Founded by authors Stephanie Pickup and Marlene Lee, the project is a partnership led by the Military Family Research Institute (MFRI) at Purdue University.

Heroes' Trees are adorned with handmade ornaments featuring photographs of military service members or drawings that represent service members. While the trees have been placed in local libraries in Indiana, schools are also appropriate places for the trees–allowing students to pay tribute to heroes in their lives and to learn about the role of the military in U.S. history.

The project is non-controversial and all-inclusive, explains Kathy Broniarczyk, the director of outreach for MFRI, because the servicemen and women honored don't have to be current members of the military. They can be someone's grandfather or uncle or a long-deceased relative who served in a past war. The project raises awareness of the sacrifices that have been made by service members and their families and creates opportunities for a variety of learning experiences for students.

Example of a Heroes' Tree Ornament

In addition to the literal trees placed in libraries and other places where members of the community gather, a Virtual Heroes' Tree has also been created to serve as a web-based extension of the project, allowing anyone to take part in viewing information on the members being honored and to learn about their service.

As part of its resource guide, the MFRI has also compiled an extensive list of ideas for school and community programs involving children and youth. Many would be appropriate for school service-learning projects or for helping children understand the death and military service of someone in their own family. They include:

- Taking a graveyard exploration trip and writing down information from a tombstone of a deceased veteran.
- Using library genealogy resources to investigate and collect biographical information on living local relatives of the veteran, and then interviewing the relatives to learn more about the service member's military experience.
- Creating family trees that make note of any relatives who served in the Armed Forces or in military branches of other countries.
- Identifying the needs of veterans in local nursing homes and Veterans' Administration hospitals and brainstorming ideas for helping them.
- Interviewing veterans about their military service, any memorable stories, their job in the military, and whether they served during a war.

To access the resource guide, view the Virtual Heroes' Tree and learn more about the Heroes' Tree program, visit: http://www.cfs.purdue.edu/mfri/public/oht/Default.aspx

CHAPTER 5

Using Information to Improve Schools for Military Students

Schools consistently use test data to determine how students are performing academically and whether some may need extra help. But educators and school officials are also interested in some of the nonacademic factors that can affect children's learning and their attitudes toward school.

The environment in which students go to school every day has been found to have an effect on how they learn. A student who feels that the adults in the school care about him is more likely to feel positive about learning than a student who doesn't feel supported. Students who are experimenting with drugs or alcohol are likely to begin having trouble academically. And those who are afraid of being teased or hurt by a bully are going to have a harder time concentrating on school work.

School climate surveys are an example of collecting and using data to improve schools. They help to show the strengths and weaknesses in each school and district, and can identify issues of concern to students and parents. They can also show whether these issues change over the year, and in what direction. Identifying areas and groups that require attention is an essential component in planning school activities, programs, and the allocation of resources. Surveys that reflect the voices of many members of the school community can help put the school on the right course.

Your child might be asked to take a survey about issues such as school safety, drug or alcohol use, or other important topics. The results of these surveys can help schools identify the needs among students and how they should be planning their efforts to help students

overcome obstacles to learning. These surveys—
in almost all cases—are anonymous and, there-
fore, not used to assess individual children or
identify particular students who may need help.

As a parent, you will receive a request to
allow your child's participation in the survey. Sometimes you are expected to sign a consent form, and in other cases, especially with older
students, you are asked to return the form only if you don't want your
child to take the survey. We would encourage you to allow your child
to take part in these surveys. The information collected has the potential to make a significant positive impact on your child's school.

In addition, as part of these school climate and behavior surveys,
parents are often invited to complete companion questionnaires so
the survey administrators can compare what students and parents
have to say. You may think that filling out a survey is a waste of your
time, or that no one is going to pay any attention to your answers. You
may also have questions about how the information will be used. But
these surveys are an opportunity for you to give the school feedback
on what you think is important.

If your school doesn't conduct these surveys, you can encourage
school administrators to begin doing so in order for the school community to gain valuable information on the experiences of students,
staff, and families, as well as their ideas on how to improve the school.
Parent leaders can create opportunities for these voices to be heard by
school administrators and work toward school policies and practices
that reflect this important feedback.

FOCUSING ON MILITARY STUDENTS

In the past, public schools generally have not considered the unique
issues and challenges facing children from military families. If they
were asked to take surveys at their schools, they were not asked to
identify whether or not they were from a military family, so school
officials have not been able to tell whether their concerns or strengths
were different from those of other students.

Because of the long wars in Iraq and Afghanistan, however, researchers and policymakers have recognized that schools should be more aware of how growing up in a military family can affect a child's education. Government leaders are recommending that education agencies examine both academic and nonacademic trends regarding military children, just as they would any other subgroup. Since most children in military families attend regular public schools, it is important to both identify their needs and put resources in place to respond.

Again, you may have questions or reservations about participating in a survey and whether the results will reflect poorly on your child's school or on military families. But these responses can help clear up misconceptions that teachers, administrators, and non-military families might have about military children. They can also be used to lobby for additional funds for hiring counselors or offering tutoring programs.

One of the first states to begin collecting information from military families was California. A "military-connected school module" was added to the California Healthy Kids Survey. Now all military parents can respond to the survey and share with district and school staff the extent to which they feel respected in school, how well the school addresses their children's needs, and their thoughts on the school's social and academic climate. Other states have since made similar efforts. In each case, individual students are not identified and the information is used to provide additional support.

USING OTHER METHODS

Sometimes schools use other methods to gather information from students and parents that can't necessarily be captured on a paper answer sheet or a computer screen. These methods allow for more feedback and conversation. For example, you might be asked to participate in a focus group about school policies, programs, or issues your child is facing at school and at home. Some focus groups also involve students.

A special type of focus group is called a Student Listening Circle, also known as the "fishbowl." This method is a chance for students to make improvements in their school. In schools that use this approach, the adults have remained committed to implementing the changes suggested as a result of the process.

The listening circle includes eight to ten students who respond to five or six questions based on survey results. Roughly the same number of adults is chosen to listen to what the students have to say. Three simultaneous listening circles are often held as part of a forum. One focuses on the role of the family, another on the role of the school, and the third on the community.

As a result of this strategy, tangible improvements have been made based on the feedback provided by the students. For example, in one school, students complained that they often had tests in more than one subject on the same day. In response, a more manageable schedule was created to avoid those situations. In another school, students complained about the condition of the restrooms. So administrators made sure they were promptly cleaned and regularly stocked with toilet paper, paper towels, and soap. In a third school, a mentoring program was created involving not only teachers but also other school staff members.

Mapping is another method used to identify issues that could be causing problems for students at school—in this case, locations on the campus where problem behavior, such as bullying, fights, or drug and alcohol use, might be more likely to occur. Mapping can also be used to pinpoint areas and times that make students feel safer and happier in school. This technique is intended to include everyone—students, teachers, and other staff members—in providing their perspectives on where such spots are located in the school, at what times of day the behavior occurs, and who is present when it happens. An important part of the process is gathering each person's theory on why specific times and locations within the school are more prone to these situations, and then following up with solutions to alleviate the problem.

Schools that have used the mapping process to address issues of violence or bullying in their schools have found it to be effective. For example, one high school learned that fights were occurring among 11th and 12th graders right outside a gym immediately after school. Students and teachers agreed that the visible presence of school staff should be increased in and around the parking lot for 20 minutes after school.

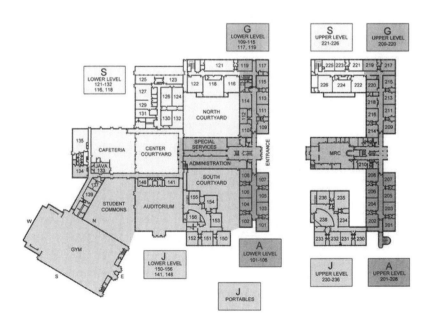

In another school, students reported during the mapping process that they felt unsafe near the school gate at the end of day. The information was relayed to the principal, who then observed the flow of traffic through the gate, making sure she was not noticed by the students. After a couple of observations, she concluded that since only one gate was open, the clustering of students trying to exit the gate all at one time led to pushing, shoving, and skirmishes among impatient students. As a solution, she simply opened up another gate to ease the congestion.

CONCLUSION

Schools and districts regularly collect information on a variety of achievement and other student indicators. But that's often where the process stops. School climate, safety, health, and behavior surveys can also provide valuable information that can be used to improve the learning atmosphere for students. As a parent, you can contribute to improving public schools for military students by taking advantage of opportunities to offer your feedback and opinions on issues that matter to your child.

Index

About the Authors

Ron Avi Astor, Ph.D., is the Richard M. and Ann L. Thor Professor of Urban Social Development at the School of Social Work and Rossier School of Education at the University of Southern California. His past work examined the role of the physical, social-organizational, and cultural contexts in schools related to different kinds of school violence (e.g., sexual harassment, bullying, school fights, emotional abuse, weapon use, teacher/child violence). Most recently, his research has examined supportive school climates in military-connected schools.

Linda Jacobson is the editor and writer for the Building Capacity project in the School of Social Work at the University of Southern California. She is a longtime national education reporter and has specialized in writing about early childhood education, state policy, teaching issues, and education research.

Rami Benbenishty, Ph.D., is a professor at Luis and Gaby Wiesfeld School of Social Work of Bar Ilan University and the head of research and evaluation at Haruv Institute. His past research includes numerous published studies on school violence and children, youth at risk, and the implementation of a large-scale school violence prevention model in Israel. Dr. Benbenishty is also an advocate of children's rights and serves on numerous public committees addressing children's needs and rights.

Julie A. Cederbaum is an assistant professor in the School of Social Work at the University of Southern California. Her research is focused on social work and public health practice with families, with an emphasis on how parents can influence adolescent risk reduction through increased relationship satisfaction and parent-child communication.

Hazel R. Atuel, Ph.D., is a research assistant professor and project manager of the Building Capacity Consortium. She is a social psychologist and program evaluator, and has expertise in the areas of health disparities, social identities, stereotyping, prejudice, and discrimination. She has managed several large-scale, federally funded projects, including San

Diego Unified School District's Safe Schools/Healthy Students initiative and the San Diego Navy Experiment, funded by the Department of Defense in collaboration with the National Institute of Mental Health.

Tamika Gilreath, Ph.D., is an assistant professor in the School of Social Work at the University of Southern California. She has worked on several projects related to substance use including biomedical studies of smoking patterns and performing secondary data analyses of the correlates of smoking among African American youth and adult samples. Her primary research interests include health disparities and patterns of co-morbidity of substance use, and poor mental health among African American youth.

Marleen Wong, Ph.D., is a clinical professor and assistant dean for Field Education in the University of Southern California, School of Social Work. She has been called the "architect of school safety programs," for her work in developing mental health recovery programs, crisis, and disaster training for school districts and law enforcement in the United States, Canada, Israel, and Asia. Formerly, she served as the director of crisis counseling and intervention services for the Los Angeles Unified School District.

Kris M. Tunac De Pedro, Ed.M., is a Ph.D. candidate at the Rossier School of Education, University of Southern California. His research interests include school climate, data-driven decisionmaking, the use of epidemiological research methods in educational research, and military-connected schools.

Monica Christina Esqueda is a Ph.D. student at the Rossier School of Education at the University of Southern California. Her research interests include emerging student populations, student experiences, and the impact of national-, state-, and local-level policies on student experiences.

Joey Nuñez Estrada Jr., Ph.D., is an assistant professor at the College of Education, San Diego State University. His research interests include school violence, street gang culture, school-based intervention, resiliency, and youth empowerment. His work has been published in major academic journals and he has presented his research at various conferences. He is currently conducting research on the risk and protective factors for gang-involved youth within school communities.